STEPHEN H. BORNMAN, CLU
Route 2 Box 311
Syracuse, Indiana 46567

The American Century
of
John C. Lincoln

The American Century

of

John C. Lincoln

by RAYMOND MOLEY

Duell, Sloan and Pearce
New York

First edition

 An Affiliate of
Meredith Press

Library of Congress Catalogue Card Number: 62-8515

Manufactured in the United States of America for Meredith Press

Van Rees Press • New York

TO THE MEMORY
of
JOHN WILLIS LOVE
WHO SHOULD HAVE WRITTEN
THIS BOOK

Contents

vii

CONTENTS

Illustrations

following page 116

Foreword

Six years ago I suggested to David Lincoln that the children of John C. Lincoln should provide the information necessary to present to the American public an account of the life, the achievements, and the character of their remarkable father. It seemed to me that such a recital would be an important chapter in the luminous history of a nation that has attained maturity in the century since the beginning of the Civil War. It might also serve as a fitting tribute to the memory of a great American as well as an inspiration to a generation that should not lose sight of its traditions.

Fortunately, a distinguished journalist and widely informed student of American business and industry was available in Cleveland, where John C. Lincoln began his active life. John W. Love undertook the task and spent two years gathering information and compiling notes. Fortunately, too, Mr. Lincoln was living and in the full vigor of his ninetieth year. From Mr. Lincoln and from his living contemporaries, Mr. Love gathered invaluable information concerning the earlier years of Mr. Lincoln's business associations and of the Lincoln antecedents and family. Pertinent data were also gathered by Professor Elmer C. Gehlke of Western Reserve University.

The tragic death of John Love terminated his work at the point where the writing of the biography was about to begin.

I then undertook that task and, with certain assistance which I shall acknowledge, composed this book.

My indebtedness to those who made my task possible is considerable. The Lincoln family, notably Mrs. John C. Lincoln, were most helpful. Charles G. Herbruck, who is associated with the Lincoln Electric Company, helped me with the highly technical aspects of the development of the products that distinguish his company and with the account of the growth of that institution to its present status.

Harold Neely, who was associated with Mr. Lincoln in the establishment and development of the Universal Wire Spring Company, told me that story. Robert B. Piser of Phoenix gathered the material on the activities of Mr. Lincoln in Arizona. Jack Stewart told me the story of the Camelback Inn in Phoenix. William H. Bemis and Frank L. Snell, the Lincoln attorneys, assisted not only in providing information but in checking the manuscript.

My son, Raymond Moley, Jr., assisted in editing the chapters and in the composition of the historical preludes.

From the beginning to the end my assistant, Marjorie Wilson, provided substantial editorial service.

It hardly needs to be said that in describing and appraising a career that extended into so many decades and touched such manifold interests there will be shortcomings in judgment and emphasis. For these I bear the full responsibility.

RAYMOND MOLEY

New York, 1962

The American Century
of
John C. Lincoln

Prelude to Chapter I

N O OBSERVER of the United States from another and less exciting planet could understand our abundant but contentious life without some consideration of our restless past. From generation to generation, from the Spanish conquistadores to the latest immigrant, there has been a process of natural selection that has determined the nature of the newcomers. America has drawn those who either found their homeland hatefully oppressive or were dissatisfied with their lot and had the energy to do something about it. The meek, the submissive, the indolent, and the resigned remained behind. From those who left their homelands have come not only our internal dissensions but our unique dynamic of progress.

For our purposes here we need not recite the story of the generations of unrest but steady growth prior to the 1840s. In that memorable decade, the fervor of independence and liberty which had already involved two armed conflicts with the mother country and had challenged the great powers of Europe burst forth with vehemence. American minds were inflamed with the conviction not only that we were chosen by destiny as a special people whose democracy was most pure and whose purposes were most just, but, by Jove, that we were militarily unconquerable and irresistible. We first challenged England again over the Oregon boundary in the form of the "fifty-four-forty-or-fight" ultimatum; our powerful slaveholding and cotton producing civilization waged a successful war of conquest against Mexico. It was our "manifest destiny," we believed, to push not only farther south beyond the Gulf and Caribbean, but over the Pacific to Asia. Historians have noted that if we had escaped civil war over slavery, we might have embarked upon a vast career of empire-building by 1860.

Meanwhile, our internal development was in full tide. Manufacturing and shipping flourished in the East, while the production of cotton brought riches to the South. The Midwest, with a rapidly growing population and rich soil, prospered. Chicago itself was a hamlet until the decade of the forties. Beyond Chicago, settlers pushed through to Oregon and California. The thrifty, energetic Mormons fled from persecution to a new life in Utah.

Freedom of choice—economic, social, and political—sparked and energized the American people. While they prospered in material things, they zealously sought reform among themselves. The era of the 1840s and 1850s was a time of "movements." Our Puritan traditions were rekindled. There were the Owenites, who found perfect consistency between socialism and Christianity. Robert Owen summoned a "World Convention to Emancipate the Human Race from Ignorance, Poverty, Division, Sin and Misery." Emerson wrote that almost anyone in the street could produce a new community project from his waistcoat pocket. A crusade for women's rights was under way. Religious dissent was rampant. And there were even movements against religion itself.

Greatest of all among the causes for social reform was the antislavery movement. While slavery had been a political issue for many years, the subject became a grave peril to peace in the 1850s. A little time was bought by the Clay Compromise of 1850, but trouble broke forth in 1854 when Kansas and Nebraska were admitted to the Union. *Uncle Tom's Cabin* appeared in 1852. Fury against the Fugitive Slave Law broke out in a state of terror in Kansas, and "God's Angry Man," John Brown, moved from that battlefield to a wild attack upon Harpers Ferry. Defiance of Federal authority was common in the Midwest. The emotional impact of antislavery stirred equally hot emotions in the South. A great fear characterized the Southern reaction, fear of an uprising among the slaves. In this burning atmosphere reason and law were paralyzed. Ultimately, war offered the terrible but inevitable solution.

Unless we recognize that zeal for reform and creative progress are both born of the spirit of liberty, it will seem incredible that the 1850s saw materially in our economy and culturally in literature an authentic Golden Age. Nearly all of the memorable figures in American literature reached their summit in that decade—Hawthorne, Whitman, Emerson, Irving, Thoreau, Lowell, and Melville. Edgar Allan Poe, in the 1840s, wrote the greatest poetry America had seen.

Tremendous economic power was generated in the 1850s. In seven years after 1850 several new railway lines pierced the Appalachians. Pioneer inventors such as McCormick and Marsh had created the means not only of greatly enlarging the productive capacity of the individual, but of creating the need for larger and larger manufacturing establishments. The sewing machine, which came from the ingenuity of Elias Howe, Isaac Singer, and others, not only eased the lot of the housewife but ushered in textile manufacturing and greater prosperity for the cotton industry. For a brief period the United States reached greatness on the seven seas. American shipmasters were unquestionably the best in the world, and the clipper ships they commanded surpassed all foreign bottoms. Maritime trade penetrated China, and under the guns of Commodore Perry, Japan was opened to the commerce of the world. All these developments called for more iron and steel, which brought into being a great industry and notable cities.

While this growth was checked by the business of war after Sumter, the foundations of modern industrial America remained intact after Appomattox.

It is not without meaning that the father of John C. Lincoln found a homeland in America in the 1850s and was a witness to the events of that period and after.

Chapter I

THE ANTECEDENTS

THE indefatigable drive and industry in the face of many vicissitudes, the zeal for justice and economic reform, and the high respect for education that characterized the career of John Cromwell Lincoln through his ninety-three years become understandable in the light of his family heritage. His father, William Elleby Lincoln, was a minister of the Gospel—fervent, fearless, and steadfast in his convictions. His mother, Louisa Marshall, was an educated woman, of a family that played a considerable part in the educational and public life of its time. She was calm, kindly, and not only a stabilizing influence upon her husband but for many years the source of her brilliant child's early education.

A detailed account of the ancestry of the parents would interest only antiquarians. Here, a few notable items will suffice. The name Lincoln seems to have been taken from the town of origin in the Middle Ages, a small hamlet in Lincolnshire, England. Numerous families of the same name trace their ancestry to that region. Those who knew William Elleby and his children have noted certain physical likenesses to the Great Emancipator. But research fails to establish any near relationship.

William Elleby's grandfather, named John Cromwell, was a surgeon in London. In 1815 he performed a remarkable operation on a survivor of Waterloo who was carrying a bullet near his heart. The bullet was removed, and this skilled performance, before the days of anesthetics or asepsis, attracted wide attention in medical circles.

The son and namesake of Dr. Lincoln was also a physician. His children were William Elleby, Henry, and Emily. William E. was born in 1831. While his father was a member of the Church of England, the son turned to a more evangelistic faith.

England in those days and long before had provided rich soil for the virile growth of evangelism. The descendants of the separatists, Puritans, and Roundheads were everywhere. Less than a century before the conversion of young Lincoln, John and Charles Wesley and George Whitefield had inflamed the countryside with their preaching. Closely related with this revivalism was the antislavery movement. The economic and political aspects of slavery mattered little to the reformers. It was a burning moral issue, an abomination in the eyes of God. And it was quite to be expected that as the crusade against slavery succeeded, the wrath of reform should spread to the United States, where the institution of slavery was an established legal reality.

When William E. Lincoln was nineteen or twenty, he had an experience that was to determine the entire course of his life. American preachers were finding eager audiences in England at the time. One of these was Charles Grandison Finney, president of Oberlin College and pastor of the First Congregational Church at Oberlin. He was a famous revivalist, aggressively antislavery and anti-Mason. A very young man, the Reverend Mr. Finney preached for a time in Borough Hall Baptist

Church near the Lincoln home in London, and young Lincoln heard the American preach. At first—he reminisced much later in life—he admired the Finney logic, but later, when "his logic took fire," he was greatly moved. When Finney moved to Whitefield's chapel—eight miles from the Lincoln home— Lincoln walked a total of thirty-two miles every Sunday to hear him in the morning and in the evening. Attendance at the meetings was small at first, but the eager disciple got some tickets for the sermons on which was printed "Life, Death, Heaven and Hell," and with the aid of three friends distributed them.

When he was an old man Lincoln wrote that the attendance grew to 5,000 and that Finney, "the mighty man of God, held them and the meetings grew in power.

"We were dying of cholera, 1,000 a day in London. . . One sermon I shall never forget was on the text, 'Because sentence against an evil work is not executed speedily, therefore the heart of the children of men is fully set in them, to do them evil.' " Lincoln wrote further: "He, after 1½ hr. of service, ended thus, 'Who can wonder that God shall drive this chariot, axle-deep, in the blood of the bodies of men.' A strange thing then happened to me; the whole congregation groaned as one, the men fell from their seats as if struck by bullets, seemingly, and in reality, in agony. The President [Finney] ordered their cravats to be loosened and their friends to quietly care for them, and not to remove them. Then the sermon went on for one hour more, and at its end 600 people stood up and confessed Christ; and among them my mother, who had walked eight miles there, and then with me eight miles home."

Inspired by Finney, Lincoln made a great resolution. He would follow Finney to America as soon as he could raise the money for passage, not because fortunes in worldly things were there, or because there was any shortage of need for spiritual work in England. It was because America offered the greatest opportunity to prepare—under Finney at Oberlin —for a life of preaching.

About this time, while the necessary money for the trip was accumulating, Lincoln experienced another inspiring thought. He wrote later that "a dear friend in England asked me to read *Uncle Tom's Cabin* by Mrs. H. Beecher Stowe. I declined to use my time in novel reading, but he urged the moral idea of the book so earnestly that I consented. With weeping, I kneeled and promised God that I would never cease struggling until the last slave was free."

And so, in 1853, he arrived in Oberlin where he enrolled in the preparatory department of the college. For more than a decade thereafter, Oberlin was the intellectual and moral source of Lincoln's training.

The village of Oberlin, Ohio, and the Oberlin Collegiate Institute were both established in 1833. It is noteworthy that the village was dedicated to the "plainest living and highest thinking." The institute began as a preparatory school but soon added a four-year college course and a theological seminary, becoming Oberlin College, the first coeducational college in the United States. It became, too, the first institution of higher learning to admit Negro students.

The thinking that pervaded the college and the surrounding area was vitally individualistic. Religion received greatest emphasis. Congregationalism, sprung from English soil long before as an outgrowth of separatism, flourished in Ohio ground.

The passionate advocacy of social reform, so dominant in the mind of William E. Lincoln, arose from Finney's Congregationalism. In that faith the sanctified individual should not be content with a righteous personal life. He must impress righteousness upon others and upon the state. Social reform is implicit in such a scheme.

In those days of controversy over slavery, the cause of abolition was a major concern of divines such as Finney. From 1850 through the years leading up to Civil War, Oberlin gained nation-wide renown as a center of opposition to the "iniquitous" Fugitive Slave Law. Citizens, students, and faculty refused to recognize the law as binding: Federal authority based upon this law was not only unconstitutional but something to be resisted to the point of open rebellion. Literary societies—in one of which William E. Lincoln was a very active member—debated the issue whether there was any moral obligation to obey an unjust law.

Near the town was a "clearing station" of the Underground Railroad. Negroes, smuggled up from the South, were put in capable hands which could lead them along the way to Canada. Funds of the township were used to care for fugitive slaves. And the Prudential Committee of the college maintained a "Fund for Fugitives."

At Oberlin the young William E. Lincoln moved into an austere atmosphere. Indeed, "plainest living" was the rule of the college in those days. Professors and students gave generous portions of their time to tilling the soil and marketing crops. Housing for the student body was provided in barracks-like monuments to austerity. Living—even in terms of the time— was cheap. Male students paid ten cents a week; the women, from $4.50 to $6.00 a year. Students bought their own fuel at $1.00 a cord. Tuition for the year was $15 for men, $12 for women. Hard work and long study hours prevailed.

Students ranged far and wide, teaching and preaching—a life to which William E. Lincoln zealously adapted himself. After two years in the preparatory department there were three years in the college. Then he entered the Theological Seminary and spent two years there.

At least three intervening years show no record of Lincoln's attendance at Oberlin. Some of this time was spent in preaching in various places, including Berea, Kentucky.

An Oberlin professor, who knew of the antislavery preaching of the Reverend John G. Fee, had urged William E. Lincoln to go to Kentucky to help. The young evangelist found life in and around Berea, Kentucky, even more exciting than in Oberlin. In his reminiscences he says of the venture, "I started, determined, if I had to die, to die preaching."

With Fee, preaching was inevitable, and, considering the state of agitation in Kentucky at the time, to die was not improbable. Fee was one for whom the term "the terrible meek" might have been coined. He was a Kentuckian and the son of a slave owner. But, while very young, he broke with his traditions and became a minister with a fierce hatred of human slavery.

He and William E. Lincoln collaborated in teaching a rural school. The building was provided by a sympathetic slave owner whom Fee had interested in the project, and Lincoln was engaged by Fee to teach for six months without pay. There was preaching in the schoolhouse as well as in the surrounding country. It appears that Lincoln was there for a part of 1855 and probably during 1856 and 1857. The little school was the sprout from which Berea College grew.

It was fitting, in the light of Oberlin's profound influence upon William E. Lincoln, that he found romance there. While a student he made the acquaintance of Frances Louisa Marshall. She attended the college and graduated in 1862. She remained in Oberlin, teaching in the high school.

Louisa, as she was most commonly called, came of notable lines. There had been Marshalls in America since 1634. Her grandfather, Seth Marshall, had migrated from Colebrook, Connecticut, in the 1830s and established himself as a hardware merchant in Painesville, Ohio. Several of the family had attended Oberlin since its founding. Her father was a farmer with good land in the Painesville area. Louisa was born there in 1838, the fourth in a family of ten children.

No understanding of the influences that shaped the life of John C. Lincoln could be complete without an account of his grandmother, Roxanna Cowles Marshall. The Cowles family, like the Marshalls, constitute a notable line of Americans. One of their great interests was in education. Roxanna in her youth had studied at the seminary at Ipswich, Massachusetts, under the famous Mary Lyon who was to go on to found Mt. Holyoke College, pioneer women's college in the United States. Roxanna carried on her studies under Miss Lyon beyond the required curriculum of the seminary, for which she was awarded a certificate. Later she served as an assistant to Miss Lyon.

Despite her household duties, which encompassed the labors of a farmer's wife and the care of ten children, Roxanna taught in Lake Erie Female Seminary in Painesville, which later became Lake Erie College. Later in life she was a strenuous champion of woman suffrage.

Louisa, as a child, was taken to the old home of her parents at Colebrook, Connecticut. She later attended the Ipswich Seminary, whose president was her relative, John Phelps Cowles. Another relative was a professor at Oberlin for many years.

Edwin Cowles, also a relative, rose in American journalism to become publisher of the *Forest City Democrat*—later, after the founding of the Republican party, the *Cleveland Leader*.

Somehow—in the Marshall and Cowles families—means were contrived to give their children higher education. Two of Roxanna's brothers graduated with honors from Yale in the 1830s. Two of Louisa's brothers attended Oberlin.

Louisa, when she met William E. Lincoln, was a striking girl—tall, with brown eyes and curly hair. She was a woman of strong character. When William E. Lincoln proposed marriage she accepted because—according to her later interpretation—"Mr. Lincoln needed a fifth wheel and I decided to be it." They were married in March 1865. It was characteristic of Lincoln's impulsive nature that they were married before he had finished his course in the Seminary. Since the rules prohibited students from marrying, he failed to obtain his degree.

Lincoln had been the beneficiary of a man of substance who admired his good works, and thus he had been able to pursue his studies with only the hardship common to most impecunious young men of the time. Perhaps this good fortune enabled him to take his bride to England to visit old places and friends. The trip also included a visit to France. They returned to live for a time in Painesville.

Altogether, Louisa gave birth to ten children. Three died soon after birth. Mary, six, and Grace, four, died of diphtheria. Sadie, at about eighteen months, was fatally burned. Those three deaths came within a period of two weeks in 1877.

As the "fifth wheel," Louisa was destined to travel a rough road. She endured stringency as well as the restless, controversial nature of a strong-minded husband shunted frequently from pastorate to pastorate, and raised four children to serve a demanding faith.

Yet in all communities where their wandering took them,

Louisa was esteemed for her kind and friendly manner. And she found time to pursue social reform, for that was part of the faith. When the cause of abolition had been attained, her interests turned to temperance. In Painesville she was active in the W.C.T.U. It was said that her last telephone call, when death approached in 1918, was to inquire what the vote for prohibition had been. Another cause had been won.

John C. Lincoln was born in Painesville on July 17, 1866. He was given the name of John Henry Cromwell, the latter being a mark of respect and admiration for the Great Protector, Oliver Cromwell. John dropped the name Henry during his college years.

That summer of 1866 the couple went to a town near Columbus, Ohio, named Hope, where the senior Lincoln was officially ordained a minister in the Congregational Church. But it was a short interlude. It is apparent that William's affection for Berea, Kentucky, and his friends there was alive and urgent, for in August 1866 he wrote a most revealing letter to his old associate John G. Fee:

"Oberlin pursues me with a steadfastness which at times seems to me cruel; because forsooth I do not value her education & have freely found fault & came into collision with one of her faculty.... Brother Fee I do not ask for a professorship; show me where I can most glorify God & by his grace there I will go. I want, & still hope to come to Ky., because I love you as a colleague & with you I can do more than I can with any other man I have ever worked with.... Even as I write I have a full persuasion that I shall be with you."

The reference above is to James Harris Fairchild who had been a professor of moral philosophy in the institution for some years and, in 1866, succeeded Finney as president. No doubt the difference of opinion related to the methods by which moral precepts should be embodied in action, for Fairchild was much more of a scholar, milder in his teaching and preaching than Finney.

Lincoln's persuasion to return to Berea was fulfilled within a matter of months. Berea College reopened its classrooms in 1866 after a wartime suspension, and, either through the influence of Fee or otherwise, the Reverend and Mrs. Lincoln were engaged to teach, commencing in the spring term of 1867. Records of the Prudential Committee of the college note the Lincolns' employment:

"On motion of Mr. Hanson Mr. W. E. Lincoln & Lady were invited to come & act as teachers—Mr. Lincoln at the salary of $50 per month, Mrs. L $30."

But, within the academic year, William E. Lincoln resolved that the life of a college teacher was not his true mission. The pulpit drew him too strongly. After this brief academic experience he turned his life's energies to preaching.

Chapter II

ITINERANT CHILDHOOD
AND YOUTH

THE earliest recollection of John C. Lincoln was of a steamer trip. He remembers little of that journey northwest along the Detroit River and on through the lakes to Northern Michigan except that he was seasick. The boy was three years old, and his father had been called to a pastorate at Antrim, which is located near Grand Traverse Bay and Lake Michigan. It was a raw lumbering town when the Lincolns arrived in 1869. No doubt, this opportunity came through the good offices of William's father-in-law whose two sons, Henry and Charles Marshall, lived and carried on business in that region.

The home provided for the new pastor was a cabin in the woods, a quarter of a mile from the nearest neighbor. The boy came to know the Indians who inhabited the region. They were welcomed to the Lincoln cabin and on occasions slept on the plank floor of the small residence.

At thirty-eight, the elder Lincoln had become accustomed to rugged living, but now he and Louisa went about the business of life in a region far more primitive than Kentucky. This was authentic frontier. William Lincoln's life was hard, as it is for venturesome men in the outposts of their calling. His preaching took him considerable distances, to neighboring towns, and the demands of his faith caused him to be absent from his family frequently. John C. Lincoln recalled many years later that his parents made four different homes in northern Michigan and that neither his mother nor his father ever complained. The family was doing the Lord's work, and that was sufficient.

Until the time of the Civil War the reaches of northern Michigan were predominantly forests of uncut timber. Active lumbering moved in after 1865, and, as the land was cleared, hardy farmers chose their acres, removed the stumps, and cleared the stone, built barns and plowed the fields. Many lakes and streams marked the region, untouched except by a few sportsmen's fishing lines and boats.

While this was the setting of a rough life for his parents, young John C. remembered his days there, until he was six, as happy ones. They were filled with friends and sunshine. There were church "socials," play in the open air with neighbors' children, and adventures in the woods. He also helped his father around the house, chopping and carrying firewood, and providing water for the kitchen. At about the halfway mark of the Lincolns' stay in Michigan, on New Year's Day, 1870, a second son was born. He was named Paul Martyn—the middle name after one Henry Martyn, a famous English missionary to India.

In 1872 good fortune rewarded the Reverend Lincoln, for he was called to a really fine pulpit in Marysville, Ohio—clearly the best pastorate he ever had. It paid a salary of $1,200 a year, ministerial affluence for those days. John C. remembered that this enabled his father to buy life insurance. Never again—according to the son—was this possible.

But difficulties in Marysville cropped up and grew over Lincoln's outspoken views. Since slavery had ceased to be an issue, zealous clergymen turned to the liquor traffic—an evil to be rooted out. William was active in the Prohibition party and assailed dominant Republicans as indifferent to the moral consequences of liquor. He was, as he was before the Civil War, ardently anti-Mason. His congregation, as well as other prominent groups in the community, grew unhappy about this disturbing voice. Ultimately his position became untenable and he left Marysville forever. Meanwhile, however, John C. had a year there in the public school.

Apparently the elder Lincoln's individual convictions, always expressed in strong terms, caused trouble for him in the other pastorates he subsequently held. For his periods of residence were never lengthy. John C. recalled, years later, that his father's troubles were the product of his political and his religious views. It seemed—the son commented with some grim humor—that his father, "would first find out what his parishioners were fond of and then attack it."

It was in Marysville that John C. enjoyed his only formal schooling until he was of high-school age. Aside from this, Louisa educated him under less than ideal conditions. The family—what with traveling from place to place—was too poor to buy schoolbooks. The other Lincoln children were also taught by their mother during their early life.

From Marysville the family moved to Cleveland, where they remained for ten months. Here, by a miracle of application made easier by the state of medical education at the time and perhaps because she may have read some medical books in Marysville, Louisa Lincoln studied and took an M.D. degree at the Cleveland Homeopathic Medical College. The purpose of this was an intention entertained by the parent Lincolns to become missionaries. In the family Bible it was noted after each entry of a child's birth, "We hope a missionary." After one of these notes there was added "in Africa." None fulfilled this destiny, although they were often reminded of it as they grew up.

The fruitfulness of the marriage apparently frustrated the ambition to go abroad as missionaries. Since ten children were born to the couple, at any one time their brood was too large for a missionary board to accept.

From Cleveland the family moved to Sinclairsville, New York, a village ten miles from Lake Chautauqua. To the boy John C., then ten years old, inquiring, enterprising, and self-reliant, the time spent there was a pleasant experience. Eighty years later he clearly remembered his labors picking berries during the hot summer weeks, thus contributing materially to the family's lean larder. His attachment to this country was a lasting thing, and for many years—including the final year of his life—he returned to spend at least two weeks at Lake Chautauqua.

In 1877 the Lincolns were on the move again, this time to western Illinois. There, Lincoln held four pastorates for brief periods. One was in a town a short distance northeast of St. Louis, another at Prairie Home near Decatur, and a third near Alton. This Illinois period was saddened by the death of three small daughters. The eleven-year-old John C. carried out the responsibility of driving alone on a bitterly cold day to the nearest town for a coffin. The death of Mary, eldest of the three, was a heavy blow to the boy, for she had been his play-mate and his personal care and responsibility.

Perhaps the Reverend Lincoln's unbending conscience made

movement inevitable, for again, in 1881, the shift was on, this time to Fairport Village, a settlement near Painesville, where the senior Lincoln mounted a pulpit overlooking a small congregation. During the three years that followed John C. grew into a tall, strong, active youth. He turned his hand to odd jobs, supplementing the family income. Even at night he set lines for catfish in the Grand River near their home and became expert at hunting rabbits. These edibles constituted a considerable part of the family's food supply. One summer he worked in a brickyard, and there was a time when he cared for a neighbor's livestock.

Shortly after their return to Ohio, John C. entered high school in nearby Painesville. This was a resumption of formal schooling, which had been limited to the first grade years before.

Prelude to Chapter III

IN THE twenty years following Appomattox the nation underwent economic and social change, perhaps more dynamic than that of any period of twice the duration anywhere on earth. It was a time flavored with vivid political happenings and transformation. It was a time of upheaval, of great undertakings and failures, of prosperity and trouble, of brilliance and baseness, of low morals among public officials mixed with high idealism, of efforts to keep and to increase what was gained and strivings to alter the way gains were made.

Civil war had smashed entire regions and the lives of many men during those four years of waste and slaughter. Yet out of the war there seemed to come a new approach, an attitude in the country that there was a pressing necessity to make up for lost time. It opened the way for a fresh surge of progress.

The nation's great leaders, before and during the war, shone on the political stage. Their performance was climaxed by a tragedy of Grecian proportions. And now, in 1866, it was almost as if the best minds and talents—the country's natural leaders—chose to avoid public office. They came forward instead to impel the industrial revolution to a fulfillment. Vision and confidence, inventive genius, business capability, and a capacity to grasp and push vast industrial undertakings marked this generation of leaders.

Conditions were auspicious. The ingredients of an enormous rise of industry and manufacturing were present in abundance and fortuitously accessible. If they were not, it was certain that what was at hand would soon make them so. Power—at first in the form of fabulous deposits of coal in the Appalachian-Ohio-Indiana-Illinois complex—was fundamentally instrumental in industry's surge. Coupled with plenty of iron ore and limestone, coal made possible the headlong expansion of railroads and steam-driven machinery. Steel became almost as cheap as cast iron, soaring from 2,600 tons in 1867 to close to a million tons in 1879.

The front of westward advance, halted while the nation's energy expended itself in years of war, moved with astonishing acceleration. Brilliant minds and strong backs, rails and locomotives soon brought two oceans a week apart. Massive investment turned the country east of Chicago into a complex of rail lines and spurs.

Business and manufacturing struck out successfully in all directions. Besides boundless natural resources, their inventive and managerial leadership counted upon a labor force marked by high native intelligence, and a market for manufactured goods nurtured by a relatively high standard of living, westward expansion, and adequate communications. Even the South, its civilization pulverized by war and neglected during the early days of Reconstruction, eventually shared the contagious progress.

One serious economic development slowed this headlong movement. In 1873 European financial supports of enormous speculation and overinvestment were withdrawn and American bankers, up to their chins in the financial tide of the times, could not take on the added load. Jay Cooke's banking house failed with shattering effect. Its own unbridled investment had been in railroad building, and its crash triggered a financial panic which was followed by a five-year depression. Thousands who had been in ventures other than land and rails suffered. Business enterprises, launched confidently on the calm financial swell of earlier years, were swamped or went under.

But the depression was not so severe or pervading as that following 1929; rather, it was typical of financial troubles of the nineteenth century, caused in large part before the Civil War by land speculation and later by overzealous railway expansion. Hardship was indeed present. The ranks of the unemployed lengthened, while among manufacturers and businessmen there were many bloody noses and cracked crowns. Weaklings of the industrial world were eliminated, leaving only the more efficient, better-managed, and stronger firms. Consolidation commenced. The growth of Standard Oil is one striking example. Formed in 1870 under John D. Rockefeller, who was to pioneer the trust movement of the late years of the century, Standard of Ohio managed, in 1878, to cement an alliance which controlled nearly all oil transportation in the nation and ninety-five per cent of refining. Petroleum production, incidentally, from just before the Civil War to about 1890, increased almost a hundredfold.

Still, there was resiliency in manufacturers and businessmen. For the record shows that the more able came back with enthusiasm and optimism tempered only by a realization that their enterprises would have to be on a narrower and more solid basis. Smoke poured forth over Pittsburgh and other smelting cities as never before; railroads fingered out apace.

At the Centennial Exposition in Philadelphia in 1876 displays in Machinery Hall presaged an era of engines and electricity and bore testimony to an unquenched faith. There stood the remarkable Corliss engine. Bell's "telephone" had yet to utter a clear word, but two years later the first exchange would be opened; by 1887, 170,000 telephones were installed in American homes and business establishments. There, too, were many sewing machines, a welcome addition among the American housewife's possessions and the backbone of a thriving garment industry. Advances in textile looms had turned quiet New England villages and crossroads into busy mill towns. Edison's telegraphy had approached perfection by this time. He was to go on to the invention of the incandescent lamp and its improvement within three years. The ingenious electrical equipment at the Exposition—part of a multitude of products flowing from factories, machine shops, and metal works of the East and the amazing Midwest—produced unprecedented improvements and production.

This vigorous story of a nation in transition contained its bleaker chapters. Underlying them were several causes. One was downright rascality in high places, public and private alike. Some of this may be attributed to a moral relapse that follows most "great causes." Then, too, the people were preoccupied in their own scramble for a share in the prosperity and lacked the measure of keen vigilance that seems to accompany adversity in our republic. Farmers, who were soon to raise the cry against government and creditors, at the beginning of this period overextended themselves, mortgaging what they had in order to acquire more in the way of land, tools, and equipment. Then there were areas of public interest, ceded to business and industrial groups in their forward rush, which had yet to become subject to legislation or the rulings of courts.

Unquestionably politics and government had facets that vegetated in the strange, unhealthy financial atmosphere surrounding certain undertakings. There were public officials abusing their public trust, implicating themselves in shady transactions and maneuverings, openly or covertly consorting with stock manipulators. There was corruption in high and low office. Graft was commonplace in the Federal government and certainly accompanied the rise of the cities, where "Tweedism" became a byword. There were scandals in outrageous diversions of government funds. The "pay-off" seemed to be the order of the day.

Economic depression and outrage at disclosures such as those concerning the Crédit Mobilier—in which it developed that shares of this construction company for the Union Pacific had been distributed by a congressman to prominent politicians, including the Vice-President, with no payment involved —moved the people to strike out at the dominant Republican Party. The House was swung from a heavy Republican majority to a considerable Democratic majority in 1874. Continued reports of corruption and unrest in the debtor-West where farmers, unable to meet their mortgage payments, clamoring for greenback inflation very nearly gave the Democrats the White House in 1876.

A season for change had come. Reformers and reform groups whiffed the air and scented their opportunity to introduce their cleansing programs. The Grange moved successfully against railway abuses and gained regulation. There was loud shouting for innovation, all the way from "free silver" to socialism. And Henry George and his concepts about the public's stake in land values became popular.

Public pressure would not be denied, and most reform came by the hand of public officials who recognized their responsibility or the expediency to act. Civil Service was pushed and laws were enacted before the period closed. But hard money held firm, and the West, defeated in this, was left to fight another day.

Twenty years after the last Civil War banner was furled—never to fly again over a charge and perhaps relegated to stand in the marble hall of some state capitol—soldiers who had marched beside it could look back with wonder at the intervening years. A spring tide of industrial achievement had paralleled the opening and subduing of the entire West. The best lands, from the western borders of Kansas and Nebraska all the way to the Pacific, were staked out and "civilized." The Indian nations were overpowered. The day of the open range had come and gone.

And the period had seen manufacturing overtake a booming agricultural production as the greatest source of national wealth.

Chapter III

THE TRAINING OF AN ENGINEER

His three years in Painesville High School worked on John C. Lincoln's intention and resolve as photographic baths on a sensitive paper. His purpose was fixed—to make electrical engineering his lifework. From his physics and mathematics teachers and the books available to him—individuals obviously competent in their calling and volumes which, to him, must have seemed a rich library—his agile and penetrating mind clearly discerned electricity's potential. The wonders of electricity harnessed to the needs of man were creating a revolutionary change in all life.

The nearest big institution in which he could obtain more instruction was Ohio State University in the state capital. There were no material means available to the family to meet his needs, but opportunity came in an offer of employment in Columbus by a farmer, W. A. Mahony, who lived on a small place two miles from the center of the city. The Mahonys, visiting Painesville during the summer of 1884, met the youth and suggested that they would provide him with room and board in return for chores about the farm.

Since Greek was required for entrance to Ohio State and it was not available in Painesville, John C. decided to take his final high-school year in Columbus. There he covered the two required years of Greek in one. Still holding his job with the Mahonys, he entered Ohio State in 1885.

While there was no specific department or school of engineering at the university at that time, the young Lincoln took all available courses which would help in his chosen profession. Most of these were in mechanical engineering. The professors with whom he took the major part of his work were in this branch of engineering—in metallurgy, mathematics, physics, and chemistry.

In those years there were a number of able men teaching these subjects at Ohio State. Another catalyst working on John C. during his Ohio State years was the friends he made among his fellow students. A notable number were to go on to make their marks in engineering, science, and the industry of America. There was, in fact, a great fund of inspiration provided for the career that he so eagerly anticipated, and his recollections later were altogether favorable to his training there. The engineering school at Ohio State was not to be established until 1895.

Lincoln's work for his upkeep by the Mahonys—together with what odd jobs he was able to get from others—did not seriously hamper his engineering preparation. Hard study and application assured him a full measure from his courses. During his final year—thanks to other jobs and occasional small sums from home—he was able to move from the Mahonys' and take a room in the dormitory at the University.

But the third year was to be his last of university life. For one thing, in 1888 Lincoln saw no reason why he should try for the Bachelor of Arts degree. That would have required courses in French and geology, subjects not specifically pertinent to his ambitions. Further, he had read practically everything available about electricity in the Ohio State library. These were of limited value to him. The art and science of engineering were undergoing such miraculous changes that by the time a book on the subject was written it was obsolete.

And so at the end of his three years he decided to leave the campus and cast his bread on the waters of industry.

It should be noted that twenty-five years later, in 1913, the university extended him the unique honor of giving him a degree of Electrical Engineer in Mechanical Engineering, *honoris causa*, predated to 1888.

In other ways his university brethren did not forget him. In 1921 a chapter of the honorary engineering fraternity of Tau Beta Pi was established. As is customary when a chapter is created, the list of graduates of the past is combed over for names worthy of election. In 1931 a group of these select engineers was admitted, including John C. Lincoln. A letter from the treasurer of the Ohio State chapter in 1956 gives the reasons for the honor:

"Mr. Lincoln was included in this group because of his outstanding achievements as an engineer, inventor, and organizer, and for his well-known character, and his relationship with his employees. We have always looked with pride on Mr. Lincoln and are happy to have him as a member of our organization in the world."

When John C. left Ohio State he gravitated to nearby Cleveland, an important center of the new electrical industry. Through a cousin of his mother, Peter M. Hitchcock, Lincoln obtained a position with the Brush Electric Company. This was the creation of Charles F. Brush, a great name in American industrial history. The plant was one of the largest enterprises in Cleveland and still growing. Three years earlier a historian had written, "Cleveland, the home of Brush, is the largest manufacturing city for electrical apparatus in the world."

It may be said that John C. Lincoln's education in a formal sense went on for at least three years more, although he was getting compensation for his work. He could scarcely have been more fortunate in the caliber of his teachers or in the opportunity of his position. Two men by whom he was employed were not only remarkable pioneers in electricity but were, in a very real sense, educators.

Charles F. Brush was one. The electrical industry was then so new and developing so fast that turning out skilled men was as important to the manufacturers as their material product. Customers required people trained for installation and operation of the equipment. Brush—to meet this demand—had established a training course for his promising employees. John C. was enrolled for this instruction. It consisted of factory work in assembling, winding, and testing dynamos and arc lamps. Ten or a dozen young men worked side-by-side with John C., and they were paid ten cents an hour, a munificent sum for the son of an impoverished minister.

Other companies were coming up with similar training courses. The Thomson-Houston plant in Lynn, Massachusetts, drew promising young men from a wide area for its "Expert-Training Department." Graduates of colleges and universities appeared among the trainees who had found their more or less theoretical education severely lacking when confronted with the realities of industry. Trained, these men were kept either by the parent company or supplied to important customers. In most cases this was shrewd business practice, for once a "graduate" was in a strong position with a customer, he was likely to favor the manufacturer who had provided this education.

John C. met Brush, but saw him only occasionally in the course of his employment. For Brush, as was true of John C. throughout his later life, applied his genius to invention rather than administration. Both were essentially pioneers rather than production executives.

A little less than a year after joining the company, John C. was introduced by Brush to Sidney Howe Short of Denver, a young man destined to attain fame in the electric-railway field. Short immediately employed the young apprentice, who was to find this connection richly rewarding in experience.

"Professor" Short, as he was generally called, was not only a promoter but an educator. At this first meeting Short was thirty years old. At Ohio State he had been a brilliant student and faculty assistant. Immediately after his graduation the University of Denver had offered him a professorship of physics and chemistry. There his interest left chemistry and concentrated on physics, and before long he was deep in research and development in arc lighting and electric traction—fields in which he took out numerous patents.

In 1885 Short left the University to join a Denver manufacturing company. Two or three years later he obtained a project for building an electric street railway in south St. Louis. His job was to supply the electrically propelled trucks for cars which had hitherto been drawn by Missouri mules. Short was financed by loans from a man he knew in Columbus, who arranged with Brush for him to buy motors and dynamos made to his specifications. Brush provided Short with space to do experimental work and to set up necessary specifications. The new employee, John C. Lincoln, was sent to St. Louis to work on the installations. His pay was fifteen cents an hour, just about the common labor rate in northern cities.

Short was a sharper businessman than his supplier. The contract with Brush proved to be profitable only to the customer. This is not surprising, since dynamos and motors were a sideline to the Brush specialty of arc lighting. But always, when promoters of electric street railways came to him, Brush provided room for their experimentation.

Short had started production with motors connected in "series" rather than "parallel." He was quick to change, however, when a former assistant to Thomas A. Edison successfully installed a system in Richmond, Virginia, in "parallel." The system came into universal use.

This is an incident illustrative of the phenomenon of progress familiar to all ages. The process was especially notable in the period we are considering, when invention followed close on the heels of invention, when changes appeared to tumble over one another across a wide, advancing front. The dynamic of the time lay in such men of vision and adaptability as Short —inventing, adapting, borrowing, improving; failing sometimes, but profiting from their own and others' mistakes. This is why it is so difficult to attribute any single instrument of progress to an individual. Progress, on the other hand, may be traced to the few extraordinary people who lead the way.

Short was not only inventive and practical, but he was his own salesman and a good one. Many prospective customers were persuaded to contract with Short after witnessing demonstrations he conducted in cities where he had an operation under way. Often in these promotions John C. Lincoln acted as his assistant.

On the Short job in St. Louis young Lincoln received considerable publicity from a sensational and very narrow escape from death. Word had come in by telephone that a trolley line had fallen a mile from the powerhouse. There it posed a sparkling threat of death. A mule had walked into the hot wire and was promptly electrocuted. John C. arrived on the scene with a hatchet he had obtained from a nearby firehouse. There lay the mule, dead on its side. The trolley was empty, and the wire dangled from the overhead line to the street below. John C. climbed to the top of the car to sever the wire.

When he chopped, the wire broke more quickly than he had anticipated. He felt current flow through his arms and shoulders with paralyzing effect. He was unable to let go, and his life was ebbing fast when his mind moved him to jump from the car to the ground, thus breaking the deadly circuit.

Newspapers headlined the exploit, "Tougher than a Mule." The durable young man continued the day's work.

John C. Lincoln's work with Short developed into a North American odyssey. After St. Louis his work took him to Muskegon, Michigan, putting six or eight cars into operation; the next assignment—Indianapolis for four; then to Columbus to install a line from High Street to the fairgrounds; followed by operations in Cincinnati, Pittsburgh, Covington, Kentucky, and Parkersburg, West Virginia. In Columbus, as in other cities, the Short contribution was essentially a continuation of existing lines.

Finally, in 1891, John C. was assigned to the biggest project ever undertaken by Short, the installation of an entire city system in Rochester, New York. It involved as many as seventy cars.

While in Rochester the vision of John C. Lincoln projected its first invention, an event which opened a new and greater era in the young man's life.

Chapter IV

EARLY ASSOCIATIONS
AND FRUSTRATIONS

J OHN C. LINCOLN's first patent—beginning a series which was to number fifty-four in the course of sixty-five years *— was on an electric brake for street-railway cars. It was devised on his own time when he was in Rochester on the Short project. His attorney in securing the patent was George B. Selden, who became famous a few years later as the holder of what he claimed was the basic patent on the automobile.†

Lincoln held his electric-brake patent for a while, then sold it to Elmer Ambrose Sperry. Sperry had a notable ability to deal with several problems at one time. Like a good field commander, he could apply his attention and abilities to several points on the broad front facing the forward movement of mankind. He was occupied with designing and building dy-

---

* A 55th was issued in 1961 for which he applied before his death.

† Selden, when Lincoln met him, was a lawyer in his father's office who tinkered with mechanical experimentation in a shop of his own. In 1875 he devised a machine which was known as a "road engine." His application for a patent was filed in 1879 and issued in 1895. After the patent had been disposed of on a royalty basis, a suit was brought against Henry Ford in 1903. Long litigation followed, and the court finally declared that, while the Selden patent was good, Ford's engine was four-cycle instead of the three-cycle engine described in the Selden patent.

namos, arc lamps, mining machinery, and other equipment. In 1890 he came to Cleveland with the intention of making street-railway cars. Before he was thirty he had commenced this enterprise. He then sold this business and joined the White Sewing Machine Company. While there Sperry, in his experimental department, built what he christened an "automobile." He got the name from a French magazine, and it was destined to immortality and to become the idiom of most tongues. In the same period he was beginning his study of the applications of the gyroscope. This was to bring him international fame.

Sperry paid Lincoln $500 for the brake patent. It proved to be fundamental. Employing the motor itself as a dynamo brake, it was highly effective. And the principle was widely employed in later years. Important though the device was, Lincoln estimated its value years later at no more than $3,000. (As with many more of Lincoln's creations, it came before its time.)

Early in 1892 Short asked Lincoln to go to Cleveland and take charge as superintendent of construction for the Short company. For the first time in his life Lincoln was in a position to tell others what to do. His salary was $2,000 a year.

Lincoln had an office in a building in the rear of Brush Electric, on what is now Chester Avenue. It was Lincoln's recollection that nearly half the Brush factory had been built to turn out storage batteries. But the battery business was sinking fast before the competition of the dynamo. This was the time of Brush's greatest frustration. Soon he was obliged to close up his business, and he moved to France. Again we see a great development which came before its time. For the coming of the automobile was to create an immediate and immense market for batteries.

During Lincoln's stay with Short in Cleveland, he demonstrated the Short street-railway cars for Tom L. Johnson—destined to fame not only in business but in politics, as Cleveland's most noted mayor. At that time Johnson was in street railways as proprietor of the South Side Electric Railway Company and in the steel manufacturing business as well.

While Short failed to get the Johnson business, Lincoln was indebted to Johnson because some time before he had heard Johnson lecture on the single tax. Johnson stirred in Lincoln something that was perhaps inevitably to come to the surface —an abiding concern with social ideas.

In the nine years after 1901, while Johnson was mayor and Lincoln resided in Cleveland, the city was the major center of the movement of Henry George. Lincoln saw Johnson occasionally but the two were never well acquainted. But just as Johnson had been converted to the ideas of George, so Lincoln, probably because of hearing so much of the noted economist from the Cleveland mayor, turned to the most noted of George's works, *Progress and Poverty*, which became an abiding interest for many years.

Lincoln's position with Short was terminated when General Electric bought out Short in 1893. However, during that year Lincoln had been spending a considerable time on designs of a dynamo and a motor. He also had made the acquaintance of the brothers Elliott—W. H., Emmett, and Samuel K. Born in Clarion, Pennsylvania, they were brought to Cleveland by their parents. The youngest, Samuel, had taken the Brush training course at the same time that Lincoln was there. Later the brothers established an electrical equipment repair shop. Available work was plentiful. Equipment in those days had little durability. Their shop was on the Pennsylvania Railroad near a street that is now Carnegie Avenue. Their ambition was to get into manufacturing in the rapidly growing electrical

field. Since Lincoln was at loose ends, he joined forces with
the Elliotts. To the enterprise Lincoln brought an indispensable contribution. He had designed and built a motor which
was precisely the basis their projected new enterprise required.

Lincoln went on the Elliott payroll as an engineer at a salary
of $1,200 a year. This was a considerable comedown from his
financial arrangement with Short. But the Elliott connection
gave him wider scope for his capacity for invention and adap-
tation. The job he was to do for the Elliotts was to design a
motor, not necessarily patentable, which they could market in
the rapidly growing trade of the time. Within a few months
the little company was producing and selling what it described
(in the Cleveland City Directory of 1893) as "multiplier slow
speed motors and incandescent dynamos."

The motor, designed by Lincoln, was one of the high and
narrow types common at the time. The patent aim of the Elliotts and of Lincoln was to make a product which could be
built and sold in a rapidly competitive industry. Fifty-nine
years later, Lincoln said that the motor he designed "was not
nearly so good as it might have been, but it was better than
many on the market."

Expansion of the market for electric motors developed with
the coming of central-station electric power. Customers were
of all sorts—manufacturing concerns, machine shops, and
printing plants. The time would come when overhead shafting
and belts to individual machines would end, and farsighted
engineers foresaw it.

The Lincoln motor was so satisfactory to the Elliotts that
in 1895 they elected the 30-year-old engineer president of the
company. The name was changed to the Elliott-Lincoln Electric Company, and the firm moved to a plant on Payne Avenue
along the Pennsylvania tracks. Two other men joined the board

at that time, J. E. and W. A. Crawford. It is probable that the new capital needed by the growing business came from the Crawfords' father. John C. Lincoln was cut in for a share in the ownership, the stock to be paid for out of an increase in salary. This was a common means of incentive then as now.

But something over which the individual enterprise of these ambitious men had no influence frustrated the business. In 1893 a financial panic swept the banks and, as in most depressions, the blow fell upon commerce and industry soon after. By 1895 "hard times" were upon the nation. Hundreds of thousands were idle. Ruin overtook many growing and hopeful enterprises. Gloom settled over the farms, and strange radical political movements were sweeping the Middle West and Far West. Big industries, like steel and iron, stemmed the tide. Pig-iron production reached a new high in that gloomy year. Electrical manufacturers, like General Electric and Westinghouse, managed to carry on with reduced business. But companies like Elliott-Lincoln, with only fifty employees, were in the eye of the storm. Survival was a matter of speculation.

The company continued to build the Lincoln-designed motor in six or eight sizes. The smallest stood about a foot high, the largest about four feet. In capacity the motors ran from one to 100 horsepower. Most voltages were 110 or 220, but those motors built for street railways were designed for 500. These larger units were built on firm orders, but the smaller ones were assembled for stock. This inventory required investment money, and money was very scarce indeed.

Again the Crawford family made some cash available, this time in the form of a loan. By late summer, 1895, with the depression deepening and a pattern for production in the shape of motors Lincoln had designed, the Elliotts and Crawfords took stock of their situation. They made the ruthless decision that Lincoln was expendable. He was, as he put it later, "frozen out" with only $200 for his investment of concept, brains, and energy.

Thus, twice in two years, Lincoln was out on his own after a promising start, first with Short, then with the Elliotts.

In 1891 John C. Lincoln had married. A daughter, Myrtie Louise, then a son, John Gladden, were born. Following the custom of his father, Lincoln selected a second name that was of a personage greatly admired for his zeal for religion and reform—Washington Gladden, a famous Congregational minister who occupied the pulpit of the First Congregational Church in Columbus, Ohio. In 1895 the Lincoln family was living in a house on Marcy Avenue, which is now East 86th Street, under a mortgage which Lincoln was paying off. Groceries, he recalled later, cost $3.50 a week. Later he also found it possible to give some financial help to his brother, James F., who had entered Ohio State to study engineering.

In the face of these multiple responsibilities and smitten by his second frustration in business, the redoubtable son of Louisa and William Elleby was neither embittered nor daunted. He set up a shop in a small bedroom in his home. During every minute he could spare from odd jobs, which served to keep food on the table and the mortgage paid, he used his great endowments of imagination, invention, and perseverance.

He took on any menial task having to do with electricity. One of these assignments was the fashioning of small devices for teaching, used by a man giving a correspondence course in electricity. One of these demonstrated that the magnetic field of the earth could be measured. Another task was the preparation of a small book for advertising use entitled *Practical Electricity with Questions and Answers*, written for the

Cleveland Armature Works Company. This concise hand-book ran to six editions with a total printing of 40,000 by 1911.

Another off-job that came to Lincoln in that summer of 1895 was the redesigning of a motor to suit the conditions of a cement mill in New York. His client was a young man named Herbert Henry Dow, son of the master mechanic of the Chisholm Shovel Works, a company with which Lincoln was familiar. The younger Dow had graduated from Case School of Applied Science in Cleveland the same year Lincoln had left Ohio State. As a student Dow became interested in brines found in certain wells in the region. After a brief experience with a small company he moved to Midland, Michigan, and formed the Dow Chemical Company.

The job Lincoln did for young Herbert Henry Dow paid $200. This sum provided the capital which started the Lincoln Electric Company.

Meanwhile, his work on a new motor was not easy. He was carrying on amid the bustle of activities usual in most homes. Still he had to wrench his creative talent free of distraction, for there were serious problems and mechanical knots to be untied. The intensity of his application to this job can be guessed from a remark made by his wife that the young son, coming downstairs from his father's workshop, used some strange and, to her, rather improper words.

By the time of his final year with the Elliotts, Lincoln knew that the motor he had designed for them was far from satisfying to him. In his home workshop he had roughed out a plan for a new and better motor. When he took it to the Elliott-Crawford board of directors they declined to consider its production. They were short of money and no doubt believed they could weather out the storm with the old product.

But, true to the instinct of the man throughout his life, Lincoln had put a practical vision on paper. The papers he held in his hand at the board of directors' meeting were ahead of what existed. What exists, contents, and satisfies most men never approaches the closer proximity to perfection that is the lure to the creative mind.

Prelude to Chapter V

THE United States before the 1880s was a silhouette against what was to come—a future made luminous with electricity. From flickering lights demonstrated by a few inventions and—to a limited extent—put to work in the 1870s and early 1880s, a vast industry based on motors, lamps, dynamos, systems of transmission, and a number of other developments was soon to take shape. It was to serve as an indispensable component of industrial America.

The America of young John C. Lincoln would not have been completely alien to what we now choose to call the "backward nations of the earth." The almost all-pervading darkness that followed sundown in the country invaded the cities of the time as well, dispelled here and there by the pale glow of gas lights. Up-to-date houses and small factories relied upon this illumination. And, although he had light, the city dweller had the threat of fire always at his elbow. His streets were less than what a department of sanitation or public works would point to as shining examples. Plodding horses drawing streetcars moved slowly along streets that were frequently unpaved, flanked by buildings of a few stories of elevation at most.

However, a certain eagerness, anticipation, and ambition

were everywhere evident. These qualities could be sensed and seen. They were in the gait of the people, in a man's aspirations, or in the way he kept his mind on the business at hand or in his willingness to take a chance or to gamble on what he thought would work.

In communications, electricity had made its mark long before. By the time of the Civil War, the telegraph had made the pony express a part of the colorful history of the West. In 1866 the Atlantic Cable linked the United States with England. There had been demonstrations of electricity's versatility. But an enormous gap between these truly remarkable achievements and electricity's assumption of key importance in the development of industrial America existed. This gap was to be closed by Americans in the decade following 1878.

The small array of electrical equipment displayed at the Centennial Exposition in Philadelphia in 1876 presaged the mature development of a fundamental industry. Perhaps first to transform the America described above was Charles Francis Brush. His first profoundly important contribution was in arc lighting. Hitherto the arc light had erratically illuminated a few lighthouses along the coast of Europe, and it had appeared on Paris boulevards in 1878. In 1879, when he installed his system in Cleveland, Brush had made the technical changes required to effect the marketability of arc-light systems. He had developed a new dynamo capable of supporting sixteen lamps in one circuit, an automatic regulator which kept the dynamo's current nearly constant regardless of the number of lights in use, and a lamp of improved design.

Immediately, Brush's system was regarded as a sound municipal investment. In 1879 and 1880 central stations were established in American cities including San Francisco, New York, Boston, and Philadelphia. At year's end—1880—more than 5,000 Brush lights were shining across the country, and by 1888, arc-lighting equipment from a number of companies was in wide use both for street lighting and certain large indoor establishments.

Conditions favoring this and other growth in the electrical industry were curiously American. We were a people, by tradition and choice, mobile and adaptable to swift urbanization. Expanding industry and commerce and the influx of foreign born stepped up this trait. In the ten years following 1880, Chicago doubled its population; New York soared from one million to 1,500,000; the Twin Cities tripled their size, while Cleveland, Detroit, and Milwaukee registered a population increase of from 60 to 80 per cent.

Requirements arising from such changes were patent. The cities called for light, power communications, and transportation in efficient, economical forms. Homes, offices, and factories offered excellent markets for the products of an electrical industry. Inventors and engineers at first conceived, produced, and even marketed their products. But soon men with another quality appeared who were to see to it that the public was "sold." For at this time the entrepreneur began to make his presence felt. Frequently, as in the cases of Edison, Brush, Lincoln, Sprague, and Thomson, all these abilities were compounded in one man. But as time passed, as the industry grew, as competition became more aggressive and financing and marketing more complex, the entrepreneur or manager gained business ascendancy.

The arc-lighting business was not a Brush monopoly. Almost from the start there were keen competitors. One was the Thomson-Houston Electric Company, under the brilliant leadership of Charles Coffin and backed by strong financial connections. It bought out a number of other electrical firms in the late 1880s, and in 1889 Thomson-Houston secured a controlling interest in Brush Electric, making it the most important producer of arc-lighting equipment in the world. This was one example of the merger pattern manifesting itself in American industry at the time.

It has been pointed out that after the fundamental invention and development stages of an industry are completed, the inventor-engineer steps aside for the entrepreneur, the business administrator, who is by training and nature more capable of handling the problems arising after the emphasis has shifted from invention to marketing, administration, organization, and finance. Coffin of Thomson-Houston (later General Electric) excelled in these latter fields.

But arc lighting, at the apex of popularity by 1890, soon experienced competition from a new source, incandescent electric lamps. True, dynamo capacity increased from six arc lights in 1878 to 65 in 1884 and 124 by 1894. By 1886, 140,000 arc lights were in service, and the figure rose to 235,000 by 1890. But thereafter the growth rate diminished.

The arc light had shortcomings that opened the way for the competition of incandescent lighting. Like other illuminants then in use, arc lighting could be installed only where an open flame was permissible. Furthermore, arc lights were too expensive and too intense for most indoor uses.

But it was not the competition of the arc light that troubled Thomas A. Edison when he turned his attention and energy to the problem of devising a satisfactory incandescent lamp in 1877. His invention was a contender for a position held by an established, widely accepted and proven system—that of the gas light. Edison was up against the problems of devising a lighting system that would be safer, provide a superior and more steady light, and cost no more than gas.

The principle of incandescence was known. Edison needed a satisfactory lamp. More than that, he needed a dynamo and a transmission system that, together with the lamps, would be cheap enough to make electric lighting competitive in price with other forms of illumination. By the fall of 1879 he had struck upon the carbonized bamboo filament for his incandescent lamp. Fortunately, his vision was backed by outlays of capital of some of the most notable financial and business figures of the day who had incorporated the Edison Electric Light Company a year before.

Now he must devise a feasible and economical transmission and power system. This would require a parallel circuit, permitting each use to operate a light independently of others, in contrast to the arc-lighting systems which were set up in series whereby all lights operated simultaneously, as on a Christmas tree. Within three years Edison had worked out a system of power and delivery. In 1882 he built the first "central station" at Pearl Street in New York City, distributing current to eighty-five buildings. By 1888, there were 185 Edison central stations in operation supplying 385,840 lamps. In addition, there were 1,291 isolated plants operating. A year later Edison had withdrawn almost completely from the electrical manufacturing field. His company was ably administered by Henry Villard, J. P. Morgan, and others who had amalgamated Edison Electric and three other firms as the Edison General Electric Company.

The Edison system had one outstanding weakness which the inventor refused to acknowledge—dependence on direct current. This required heavy copper wiring and was limited in distribution area to about one mile. In a city of considerable size a number of central stations were necessary. Communities of small population simply could not afford the system. A solution lay in alternating current, and it was George Westinghouse who recognized its future. The concept of alternating current originated in Europe, and an article in an English engineering journal attracted Westinghouse to the idea.

To make alternating current practicable, Westinghouse developed a modern transformer which changed voltage from a high transmission value to the low value necessary for the operation of incandescent lamps. Westinghouse's AC system also featured the parallel-connection method.

In January 1886 this versatile man formed the Westinghouse Electric Company. By fall the first AC system was manufactured, then put into service in Buffalo, New York. Within a few months twenty-five orders for AC plants were secured.

Edison stuck by his direct-current guns while Westinghouse and Thomson-Houston progressed in the AC field. By 1888 there were nearly 66 central electric systems for all purposes, and 3,000 ten years later.

As American cities experienced swift expansion, a demand also arose for cheap, efficient, and rapid means of transporting the population—workers from their homes to the shops and factories, consumers from residential areas to central business districts. This demand was met by the electric street railway.

The first successful, large-scale system was installed in Richmond, Virginia, by Frank Julian Sprague in 1888. Brush had installed a commercial railway in Cleveland four years before, but it had proved costly and was abandoned after a year. Sprague's achievement literally fired the progress of electric street-railway construction. By the fall of 1889 there were 180 systems in operation with 1,260 miles of track and about 2,000 cars. Sprague and Thomson-Houston were the key firms in this enterprise. Then in 1889 Edison General Electric bought out Sprague, and in 1890 Westinghouse entered the field.

This period also saw the appearance of motors of many sizes that were to spur a number of changes in the country, a forward thrust of manufacturing that would place the United States in the van as an industrial nation. Motor improvement was facilitated by the refinements introduced in the dynamo, and, while Edison General Electric neglected this field in the late 1880s, Sprague, by early 1887, had sold 250 motors—ranging from ½ to 15 horsepower—to clothing factories, printing establishments, and various kinds of mills. Still, the market had been dented ever so slightly. By 1890 only 16,000 out of a total of almost six million horsepower used in manufacturing was transmitted by electricity.

Chapter V

THE BEGINNINGS OF
LINCOLN ELECTRIC

For some years Lincoln had entertained the ambition of forming his own company. Then, with the frustrations of terminating associations with Short and the Elliotts, an unsubstantial dream stabilized into reality, his fancy into determination. He made the momentous decision that fall. The capital he needed was the $200 fee from Dow. The basis of his operation was the new motor.

This motor was not so high and narrow-waisted as the one he had designed for the Elliotts. It conformed in design to those coming into use at the time—circular in shape, and in diameter about the same as its height. Lincoln believed it would be more durable than earlier motors, and, in the design, he had aimed at manufacturing at the lowest possible cost. His idea of durability was vindicated, and sixty years later he ventured his belief that some of his early motors were still running.

Lincoln found the mechanism to be patentable and in 1895 took out his second patent, Number 539,277. With this new motor as a model and his $200, he opened his own shop in the

Perkins Power Block in downtown Cleveland at Frankfort and what is now West Third Street. This building in which the Lincoln Electric Company, unincorporated, was born was known as a "power block" because it was designed to provide steam power for tenants from a boiler and engine in the basement. It was built in 1882 by Jacob Perkins, a wealthy railroad promoter and the owner of considerable downtown real estate. Tenants were small manufacturers, printers, and others who needed space for machines and power to drive them. The motive power was delivered to tenants by belting which ran to overhead shafts hung from the ceiling of each story.

Ultimately, the very progress made in electrical machinery by their tenants would make such power buildings obsolete. Owners still continued to rent space to industrial people, but power came from the electrical utility company.

Within two or three weeks Lincoln found his quarters unsatisfactory. Probably they were too large. He moved his things, including a bench and some secondhand tools he had bought, to the fourth floor of another power building at the corner of St. Clair Avenue and Ontario Street. This was in the wholesale district where numerous small manufacturers were getting their starts. As they grew they built their own buildings elsewhere. But the St. Clair-Ontario address had the advantage of being at the very center of downtown Cleveland, close to prospective customers and suppliers.

Lincoln built direct-current motors with two poles, at first, of from one to five horsepower. At the new location he became acquainted with an elevator boy, Marty Madden, whom he employed as a helper. Madden remained with him for years. Some time later, as his business grew, Lincoln added another helper.

Few manufacturers could have made as modest a beginning

as Lincoln, even in those days. His practice was to call on a prospective customer, and if he found him interested in a motor he would invite him to the shop. After he made the sale, he produced the product and delivered it. Then he would invest the money for more material. He and his two helpers built the motors. Lincoln handled all buying and selling. In the evenings he answered the correspondence. On Saturdays—business days in that era—he pedaled his bicycle around town collecting from customers, ordering materials, making payments on his own debts or persuading a creditor to wait another week. He gave discounts for early payment, but under the conditions of that money-scarce time such discounts were largely academic.

Before long, Lincoln was making larger motors. And within the first year of independent enterprise he was also making generators—low-voltage and of his own design. These were not remarkable machines, but, like his motors, they were simple and durable, and as cheap as could be manufactured. Still, nine-tenths of Lincoln's output was motors. A small advertisement in the 1896 Directory described his Lincoln Electric Company as a maker of both motors and dynamos, and himself as "manager" of the company.

His first customers were in the immediate neighborhood—mostly printers, garment makers, small machine shops, and stamping plants. His first dynamo, of about six volts, was sold to electrotypers who served printers. All this time the users of electricity were moving out of the old power blocks. They became customers of the young Cleveland Electric Illuminating Company, which had consolidated with Charles F. Brush's light and power company in 1892. The day, however, was far distant when each machine in the shop would be driven by its individual motor. But in those days it was usual for a central motor to drive a line shaft and belts to the various individual operations.

Fortune had smiled on John C. Lincoln's operation for a little more than a year when another setback came. Fire severely damaged the shop. In the ruins stood several blackened machines with their belting; patterns and incidental tools were scattered about. His machines were all secondhand, and the money loss was not great. But to Lincoln at the time it was a heavy blow. He found himself back where he had started in 1895.

Lincoln's cousin, Peter Hitchcock, offered to help, but John C. decided to get by without a loan. His gratitude for Hitchcock's offer, however, was long remembered. Lincoln salvaged what he could, bought more secondhand tools, and moved across the alley to the third floor of the World Building at 71 and 73 Ontario Street. The *World* was an evening newspaper, founded in 1889. In 1907, after reorganization and a receivership, it was merged into what became the *Cleveland News*. In these new quarters Lincoln was to carry on his business for several years.

In 1896 the election of McKinley and the end of the free silver scare, through business confidence, accelerated the natural recovery of the country from the long depression. John C. Lincoln soon had made up for the disaster of the fire. Business picked up briskly. And the application of electric power from an individual power source meant a tremendous saving for all sorts of businesses. One purchase of motors by a printing establishment in Lincoln's neighborhood cut its costs fifty per cent. Manufacturers of machinery of all kinds began to install motors on their products. So, as his business grew, Lincoln was able to hire more workers and to.devote full time to sales, collecting, and even to the development of new products.

Builders and installers of elevators in the rapidly growing city began to call on him for motors and became leading customers. An elevator concern in Buffalo was one of his first purchasers of elevator motors. It was characteristic of Lincoln that he had entertained an idea of this sort of business, even before he had started his own company. His second patent, of 1895, was of a motor he assigned to L. S. Graves and Son of Rochester, who had switched from the manufacture of hydraulic to electric elevators.

The expanding market created a highly competitive atmosphere in Cleveland. Little businesses like Lincoln's were threatened by such big, national producers as Westinghouse and General Electric. Their size had been achieved by amalgamation. Short, for example, sold his company to General Electric. He then turned his remarkable energy in another direction. He joined forces with the Walker Manufacturing Company in Cleveland, a foundry and machinery concern. With Short it made an effort to get into the electric traction business—a booming line at the time. Short's ideas and energy helped the company succeed, and soon it was a formidable competitor of both G.E. and Westinghouse. In 1898 Westinghouse purchased a controlling interest in the Walker enterprise and thus gained a plant in Cleveland. John C. Lincoln's old associates, the Elliott brothers, were still in the field as were Edward S. Ford, the Ohio Electric Works, P. H. Electric, and United Motor.

The era of mergers and big business was beginning. It was a rough-and-tumble time, and it was to give William Jennings Bryan his "antitrust" issue in the campaign of 1900.

But this looming competition did not worry Lincoln. The costs of the leading companies sheltered a little enterprise like his. And he saw to it that he could undersell them.

Lincoln's home life was simple but sufficient. He was able to put aside some savings even when his business required the plowing back of profits to provide for a larger working force and more equipment. He prudently paid off the mortgage on his Marcy Avenue house, and after the turn of the century built a new residence, in East Cleveland at Terrace and Lee Roads. The family moved in 1903, retaining ownership of the Marcy Avenue property.

Though the memory of the depression had restrained too rapid expansion, by this time it was clear that a business move was desirable, and in about 1904 Lincoln moved his growing company from the World Building to the Sipe and Sigler Building at what is now 1232 West Third Street. Almost all of his business was in motors, but he turned his hand to producing a few motor-generator sets. Theodore Willard came to Lincoln for one of these machines for use in battery charging. Later, Sipe and Sigler—Lincoln's landlords—helped Willard establish the Willard Storage Battery Company which was to become one of Cleveland's leading concerns and a nation-wide operation.

Lincoln was now in his later thirties. His family was comfortably settled in the new house. His son, John Gladden, and his daughter, Myrtie Louise, were in school. His business was riding the swell of recovery in the new age of electricity. With relief from immediate pressures his mind—as always, concerned with venturesome plans—turned again to invention.

This was the pattern of his life—always to look to new horizons beyond the immediate and often alluring certainty of production in quantity of something he had already developed successfully. Mere administration or even the making of large profits could not occupy his interest. He was a responsive man, always willing to listen to a new idea or some way of improving on what already existed, always anxious to apply himself to new problems. Most of his inventions were devices or machines to reduce the cost of production or to improve methods of the operation of an existing concept. Some inventions proved to be significant, breaking new industrial ground, often providing the basis for big new businesses. Some were simply the expression of an inquiring, restless mind. Some were left behind by the sweep of technological change. Others were rendered impractical because of shifting business and economic growth.

One of his interests in this period was an apparatus for curing meat by electricity. He had this in mind in 1901, and took out a patent eight years later. For a short time in 1908 he was associated in a small way with the Electric Meat Curing Company. It did not prove practical as a major venture. Forty years would pass before the modern tenderizing process would become general.

A review of his patents shows an amazing versatility. He developed a magnetically controlled mechanism for opening doors in mines or other enclosures. He worked out a method of using the power of a motor to produce a reciprocating mechanism. Electric controllers for starting motors and electric brakes appear in his list of patents. In 1904 and 1905 he applied for several patents for improved arc lights. They contained excellent ideas, but the arc light was soon to be replaced by Brush's system of electric lighting.

The electric automobile had intrigued Lincoln. It was a luxury then enjoyed only by the wealthy or by exceedingly prosperous physicians, and he decided on an unusual method of acquiring one: he built one himself.

For a time he believed that the future of the horseless carriage lay in electrical propulsion rather than in steam or gasoline. In building his own car he had the mechanical work done in his shop. He bought batteries, tires, lamps, and a few other accessories. This electric automobile had a unique feature. Utilizing ideas from one of Lincoln's early patents, the car was equipped with a regenerative brake. Going downhill the motor acted as a brake and generated current to recharge the batteries.

For a time Cleveland was a center of electric-automobile manufacturing. Walter C. Baker, two years out of Case School, had built an electric automobile in 1893. In 1897 he turned to its production and in 1898 formed his own company, the Baker Electric Company, now Baker Industrial Trucks Division of Otis Elevator Company. An old firm of carriage makers, Rauch and Lang, entered the business shortly after Baker. Elmer Sperry produced an automobile and sold the business to the Waverly Company. In the course of the life of the electric auto Cleveland had at least ten companies in production.

Lincoln ventured onto the streets with his car early in 1904. One of his two-horsepower motors propelled it at fifteen miles an hour on level pavement. He saw that a much larger motor would be necessary for the higher speeds that the market would demand. But no battery built could operate such a motor. He kept working on the car for some years, taking a patent on the reciprocating mechanism, but he was to see the electric car reduced to rather gentle uses—for women and for physicians making calls. By 1920 it had practically vanished from the streets.

However, while it was in use, the electric automobile provided Lincoln with some profitable business. His device of a small motor generator set was suitable for service stations or for home use. It was set on a small platform, easy to fit in a garage. With a switch on the wall, the owner could attach the motor to the battery and leave it for the night. It was said "to make charging as easy as driving." By morning the car was ready for another day. Lincoln sold hundreds of these sets to customers all over the country, but by 1916 the business had faded away before the conquest by the gasoline car.

But there was a vastly important and lasting by-product of this enterprise, making possible in part the great advance of Lincoln Electric. This was the emergence of an efficient motor-generator set. It became the standard type of machine for generating electricity for arc welding. This source of power, together with the welder, surpassed the transformer-type welder. Further, Lincoln's company could produce these sets at low cost because of its lead in developing motor generators.

In 1905 Lincoln applied for two patents on designs for a variable speed motor or, as it was later called, an adjustable speed motor. It was designed to be valuable for "lathes, machine tools, printing presses, electric launches, mechanical cranes and the like." A third patent was applied for in 1906. All these motors operated with direct rather than alternating current.

One of these patent applications was witnessed by Reuben Hitchcock and another by Charles Hitchcock, sons of Lincoln's cousin Peter, an old and warm friend who had taken a paternal interest in the electrical work of his two neighbors, Lincoln and Brush. Reuben and Charles were attracted by the business possibilities of the motors in Lincoln's shop. In 1905 Peter Hitchcock and Lincoln, in partnership, formed a company to produce adjustable speed motors. Housed in the Caxton Building, this company was first known as the Lincoln Electric Manufacturing Company and was then incorporated as the Lincoln Motor Works in 1907.

Peter Hitchcock died in 1906, but his sons carried on the new motor company when Lincoln sold out his interest for $25,000. Later, the company's name was changed to the Reliance Electric Company and the plant was moved to Ivanhoe Road in East Cleveland.

With the establishment of Reliance in the direct-current-motor business, Lincoln shifted the interests of his company to the well-established, alternating-current, "squirrel-cage" type of motor, on which the original patents had expired. For a number of years Lincoln and Reliance exchanged products, the one making AC, the other DC equipment. Reliance has since become one of the nation's leading manufacturers and is famous for its adjustable-speed systems. Today it turns out heavy-duty motors, related auxiliary equipment, and control systems for both AC and DC motors.

While Lincoln extended his interests during those early years of the new century through his association with a number of companies, his own Lincoln Electric Company continued to prosper in a modest way. As it approached its tenth anniversary with Lincoln as sole proprietor, the assets behind the credit of the business, aside from the shop itself, included the three residences that he owned. He still took whatever time was allowed in meeting his bills, but his reputation was excellent. Now, he began to look beyond a single proprietorship to an incorporated company.

Chapter VI

THE LINCOLN ELECTRIC COMPANY, 1906–1914

CLEVELAND'S James H. Griswold was admitted to the Ohio bar in 1901 and launched his career in a growing city already well supplied with lawyers. The income from his practice, modest in its beginnings, was supplemented by the prosaic activity of collecting bills. Such was a common means of survival of struggling young attorneys. Among the bills for collection one day in 1906 was a statement from Sigler Brothers, Jewelers. It represented $75 owed by John C. Lincoln.

Griswold presented the bill to Lincoln in the manufacturer's shop-office. "I know about that bill," John C. commented, "and I will pay it when they give me credit for the materials I returned, as was agreed on."

The young lawyer took the bill to the Sigler people and found that Lincoln was correct. When he returned with the corrected bill Lincoln was apparently impressed by the courtesy and promptness of his visitor. He asked in a friendly manner what Griswold's business was and learned that the bill collector was a lawyer by profession and preference. "I might have some business for you," said Lincoln reflectively.

A few weeks later Lincoln called at Griswold's office and said he was contemplating the incorporation of his company and would like to have Griswold take the necessary steps. And so the Lincoln Electric Company was duly incorporated with a capital of $10,000, divided into 100 shares worth, at par, $100 each.

Lincoln suggested that Griswold take one share as his fee. The young lawyer was pressed for money and countered with the suggestion that he take $75 in cash instead. In later years Griswold had reason to regret this choice. His practice grew large, and his became a noted name in Cleveland. (His son is today Dean of the Harvard Law School.) Many years later, Griswold said that the one share he declined would have been worth $10,000. Upon hearing this, Lincoln felt the figure to be an exaggeration since "this was no early Ford company." It would, Lincoln acknowledged, have been worth a substantial sum.

"For no very definite reason" John C. put all of the stock of the company in his wife's name. "That was all I knew about business." This transfer didn't help his credit which, such as it was, continued to be respected because of his well-known honesty, energy, and inventiveness. Then, about a year later, Lincoln sold a sixth of the company for $2,000 or $3,000. The purchaser sold it back a few months later when Lincoln was possessed of some ready cash.

The summer of 1906 saw the Company energetically growing to a point where the downtown space could not accommodate its twenty employees adequately. Since his company had limited credit and no capital for expansion, John C. "had to dig up the money." He bought a piece of land from Charles F. Brush on Kelley Avenue at the corner of what is now East 38th Street. This was in the rear of a piece of land Brush had bought near his home on Euclid Avenue, then Cleveland's ultra-fashionable strip. Near Lincoln's half acre there was Brush's experimental windmill. Obviously, Cleveland's zoning restrictions were not what they are today. The sources of wealth were permitted to mingle with its sometimes ostentatious display. Perhaps there was greater tolerance then for the things that made abundance possible.

And so Lincoln planned and erected a three-story structure with a high basement, rigidly functional, designed to meet current needs. Later it was to have an additional story and a small office annex. The cost of the new plant was between $20,000 and $25,000. A half century later the building was still standing, serving a useful purpose long after the surrounding mansions had become curious relics of a robust age or had fallen before the assaults of demolition crews.

Soon after the move to East 38th Street, the work force expanded to thirty. Business was running at the rate of $50,000 to $60,000 annually. Products ranged from direct-current motors and motor-generator sets to some alternating-current motors. Most were sold to printing shops, manufacturers of women's clothing, and a few stores. Generators were also sold to plants for connecting by belting with steam or gas engines for providing lighting in places where there was no service from the public utilities. For a time motor-generator sets were in demand for electric automobiles.

In 1907, at forty-one, John C. Lincoln was a business success. He could look forward with considerable assurance. A money panic, gathering over the nation, presented no deterrent to his operations. Lincoln's company had grown from its fragile infancy into hardy youth. The sparks of invention from many minds, intent upon the full exploitation of the potential of electricity, the rapid cross-fertilization of ideas from one company to another, and the concept of mass production, dramatically brought to public notice by Henry Ford, were finding reality in many lines of manufacturing. And the country grew apace in an era of profound peace. All these augmented developments assured Lincoln a luminous future.

The period between incorporation in 1906 and the beginning of the war boom in 1914 was conspicuously formative for Lincoln's company. New specialists entered his service, young men with their eyes and efforts focused on the future and with much to add to the natural endowments Lincoln himself was able to give to his business. Lincoln welcomed such help. Indeed, within his limited financial means, he invested heavily in it. For he was giving much of his thinking to the evolution of new products and important improvements in what he had already made. Also, with growth, financial problems were more easily overcome.

His thirty employees of 1906 and 1907 grew to 70 by 1910, and to 100 by 1911. Among these were a bookkeeper, a buyer, two or three salesmen, and four shipping clerks. By 1914 the plant bustled with 150 employees. The company's business in that year reached a gross of $250,000.

Most of the production of the plant was in AC motors and battery chargers. Later, the war killed this latter product when electric automobiles were largely supplanted by internal-combustion types and luxury items were restricted. But war gave as it took away. It created the beginnings of a demand for arc welding which required a somewhat modified motor-generator.

Lincoln's major interest throughout remained in engineering rather than in what he considered the more prosaic routines of management and marketing. His early business was almost wholly in custom-made products. The customer would describe his need, and Lincoln would make an appropriate product to meet it. This was his joy and his talent.

The limitations of the company's exchequer required the maintenance of a line of credit as long as possible, although payrolls had to be met in cash. When payday came he would comb the mail for checks, stir up accounts receivable, and, if necessary, borrow a short-term sum from the First National Bank.

In 1907 Lincoln's brother, James Finney, his junior by seventeen years, entered his employ at the age of twenty-four. Like John C. and their father, William E., he towered over six feet. While studying at Ohio State he had worked for Lincoln during summer vacations. His job when he entered the company was that of a salesman—a function for which his energies and capacity admirably fitted him.

James Finney Lincoln's childhood had been passed in Painesville, where the Reverend Lincoln had finally settled down permanently. Other than the hardships of wandering, the minister's family's situation remained unchanged. The pinch of austerity, marked in the upbringing of John C., was the same. With savings from a variety of jobs in and around his home and with loans advanced by John C., James was able to enter Ohio State University in 1902. By that time O.S.U. had a full-fledged school of engineering. Charles Kettering—three years James's junior—was also a student there. And some of the same professors who had so greatly influenced and in-spired John C. were still conducting courses. Prominent among these was R. D. Bohannon, a colorful and talented teacher of mathematics. James's final year was interrupted by a siege of typhoid fever, and he was unable to graduate with his class. As in John C.'s case, he was, several years later, granted the degree with honors.

John C. was happy to have him join the company and greatly valued his aggressiveness and business sense. He was immediately put on the payroll at $150 a month with a percentage in the gross sales. As time went on, John C. moved his brother into a position of sharing both the responsibilities and results of the company's business. Later he was made vice-president with an opportunity to buy stock. This promotion was well deserved, for James F. was an energetic and efficient administrator. He was abreast of the march of progress and had noted with great interest the methods which had made Henry Ford famous in the expanding automobile business.

About this time a new, and, as it proved, sensational factor appeared in the industrial picture—arc welding—something which had occupied a corner in John C.'s teeming brain for some years. In 1909, after study, speculation, and experimentation, he became seriously interested in applying this use of electricity.

Both Lincoln brothers, each in his own fashion, were attracted by the idea of making welding machinery a part of the company's line of products—John C. by the engineering problems involved in the process and its application, James F. by its practical development for commercial production. Up to the beginning of the First World War in 1914, arc welding had received considerable laboratory attention, but, as is always the case with a revolutionary industrial development, considerable time had to elapse between discovery and commercial application.

Arc welding cast its first brilliant glare in the early 1880s when a Frenchman named Demeritens used an arc to join the plates of storage batteries. Five thousand miles away Elihu Thomson—an American, born in England—introduced the first resistance welder at about the same time. The method of joining metals by the use of electricity as a source of heat was illustrated at the Paris Exposition in 1889. In 1887, a Russian, N. V. Bernardos, had improved on the Demeritens process and received patents on a process of arc welding in which a carbon electrode was used. His process was patented throughout Europe and received note because of some dramatic repairs on steam boilers. During that period an American—C. L. Coffin—in Detroit, and another Russian, named Slavianoff, received patents for a welding process in which a metal wire rather than a carbon was used as an electrode.

Basically, arc welding was the same process in those early days as it is now. In the early experiments electric current was supplied by batteries; later, from generators and transformers. The current is carried from its source through cables to the material to be welded, where the circuit is broken by inserting into the cable an electrode sustained by a suitable holder. The electrode is a substance similar to that which is to be welded. The electrode was, at first, a piece of carbon; later, a wire. A small gap in the circuit is created by holding the electrode 1/16 or 1/8 of an inch from the metal to be welded. The electricity jumps this small gap, creating a sustained spark called an arc.

The arc is extremely hot—around 10,000 to 20,000 degrees Fahrenheit—and is capable of melting the metal almost instantly. The electrode also melts and flows into the joint being welded. When the arc is withdrawn, cooling solidifies the two pieces of metal into a homogeneous mass.

For two decades after its discovery, arc welding received little serious attention. The nature of the arc phenomenon and the metallurgical problems were little understood. The electrical requirements of the circuit were not appreciated, and good equipment for producing and controlling the arc were not available. Most of the early development was done in European laboratories, with little or no effort toward finding economical, practical ways to manufacture equipment which could be used in industry.

Welding was first used for repairing loose rivets in steam boilers which could be quickly sealed by the arc. Steel foundries could also fill holes in defective castings by depositing new weld metal. Riveted hulls in ships could be repaired in the same way.

The Lincolns were among the very few to strike into this new frontier. By 1909 John C. was able to foresee the disappearance of the electric automobile and, hence, that his charging sets were doomed. His unusual mind, compounding a first-rate grasp of the practical with great imagination, was attracted by the concept of arc welding. He conceived the idea that his motor-generator set might be adapted as a welding apparatus.

The brothers realized that their experience in making direct-current motors and battery chargers would enable them to design and manufacture equipment for welding which would give better control of the arc and be low enough in cost to attract buyers. They made their first welding set in 1909 and thus began an interest at Lincoln Electric which ultimately would surpass all the other products of the company.

While John C.'s first welding patent was still five years distant, the company put into production a machine for welding and put it on the market. At first, sales were few, but in 1911 an article appeared in the *Iron Trade Review*, noting that Lincoln Electric had introduced an electric arc welder "for purposes of patching defective castings, burning off risers and similar work in steel foundries." It was identified as a transforming device, capable of taking the high-voltage, direct current present in shops and transforming it to a low voltage that could be used for welding. The article stated that it was "fundamentally a variable voltage machine, the voltage at the arc depending entirely upon the amount of current flowing and this voltage at the arc can be set for any value which the operator may desire." This method of controlling the arc in the circuit was a significant, not to say revolutionary, development in welding. Ultimately, the first welding set made to Lincoln's specifications was to replace all others.

Most welding machines in use were large, stationary units of a constant voltage. Their construction required a team of operators to work the same machine. And if the single machine failed, the shop had to close down for repairs.

The Lincoln machine was a single-operator, portable affair which the operator could shut down when he was through with a job. Most important, he could control his own machine without going to a central station. This development made welding much more attractive to industry. Before long, sales rose hopefully and the company was offering a line of machines in various sizes for both AC and DC current. In 1912 John C. applied for a patent on the machine. It was duly issued in 1917.

This fundamental industrial development gave Lincoln Electric a lead in the field that it has always maintained, although the two giants—Westinghouse and General Electric—soon entered into competition.

Having mastered the problems of improving the usability of welding machines and the regulation of the voltage, John C. next turned to the problem of purifying the metal in the weld. In older machines and in his own the welded metal—when exposed in a molten state to the atmosphere—absorbed oxygen and nitrogen, thus forming oxides and nitrates into the substance when it solidified. This made the weld brittle.

John C. labored over the problem and soon filed an application for a patent on a process intended to eliminate this defect. The invention consisted of applying finely powdered metals adjacent to the edges and surfaces of the metal to be welded. This—he claimed in his application—overcame the "apparently inherent defect in the commercial process." He had suspected that the materials acted as a deoxidizing agent at high temperatures and that they "formed minute quantities of an alloy during the fusion of the welded metal." He was correct in his suspicions.

John C. Lincoln's experiments in welding at Lincoln Electric continued for several years. He also made significant contributions after 1914 in his work on the joining of railroad rails. Others were also searching for the answers in the broad field of welding. After more than fifteen years, electrodes which made arc welding a low-cost process that could be used in all sorts of manufacturing came on the market. The early visions and experiments with which John C. Lincoln was occupied when welding was little more than an interesting scientific demonstration thus were climaxed in a signal industrial achievement.

Prelude to Chapter VII

BY THE LAST decade of the nineteenth century it became clear that the United States was approaching a vast breakthrough across the entire front—economic, social, and political. There were appearing new forms of commerce and industry, rising standards of living, shifts in the population, and a transformation in the nature and direction of dissent and reform. In the first decade of the new century these changes took form and substance.

The roots of this growth were in industry, where brilliantly inventive minds were working at new technologies, new forms of transportation and communication, and new services for the needs of the people. Electricity provided the most dramatic manifestation of this change.

To the sensitive mind of Henry Adams, one of the great prophets of the new order, this came with terrific impact. In his *Education of Henry Adams* he tells of what he saw at the Paris Exposition in 1900:

"The dynamo became a symbol of infinity. As he [Adams] grew accustomed to the great gallery of machines, he began to feel the forty-foot dynamo as a moral force, much as the early Christian felt the Cross. In seven years [since the Chicago World's Fair in 1893 which he also attended] man had translated himself into a new universe which had no common scale of measurement with the old. He found himself lying in the Gallery of Machines, his historical neck broken by the sudden eruption of forces totally new. The year 1900 was not the first to upset schoolmasters. Copernicus and Galileo had broken many professional necks about 1600; Columbus had stood the world on its head toward 1500; but the nearest approach to the revolution of 1900 was that of 310 when Constantine set up the Cross."

There were others, less historically minded but more practical, who comprehended these changes and sought to do something about them. There were those who capitalized on the revolution and who amassed great fortunes and vast establishments. Others deplored the excesses of the new industrialism and sought to regulate and correct them by law and otherwise. Thus an age of revolutionary industrial expansion came also to be a period of social and economic reform. The former sought customers and thus to raise the standard of living of the people. Others sought a different ratio of distribution in the name of social justice, in the riches which grew from industry.

In the McKinley era the consolidation of industrial concerns, which in the Nineteenth Century were called "trusts," became "mergers" or new corporate forms. Bigness was not the result of any one factor, but at its heart was economy of management and control of the market. The laws against monopoly—except the Interstate Commerce Act—which were on the books at the turn of the century were inadequate or unenforceable. Even the Sherman antitrust act carried with it no clear definition of what was or was not permissible. Interlocking directorates and stock ownerships were put to ruthless purposes. Price wars flared with deadly effect upon small enterprises. In the name of competition there were those who were bent upon eliminating competition.

The railroads achieved immense size and strength. These were used as allies of industrial giants to eliminate weaker members. They projected their power into the politics of many states, with plenty of corruption and a moral disintegration of the political parties as a result.

Another Adams—Henry's brother Brooks—saw in this consolidation of business and industrial power a deadly peril to democracy. His book, published in the late 1890s, *The Law of Civilization and Decay*, put what was happening into a baleful historical context.

In the electrical industry, to which John C. Lincoln had dedicated his earlier business life, there was consolidation, too, although—unlike conditions in the steel, oil, and railroad industries—there were no serious evils. Technological change was proceeding in the uses of electricity so rapidly that competition still thrived. In the 1890s two electrical giants emerged, General Electric and Westinghouse.

General Electric represented a combination of Edison General Electric and Thomson-Houston. One of these companies had been foremost in the development of direct current; the other, alternating current. The merger made it possible to fuse the two in one industrial concern; the one providing for the manufacture of lighting and the other generators and transmission systems.

Westinghouse, which originated in the inventions of George Westinghouse, was in the early days a smaller company but an effective competitor. Westinghouse apparatus illuminated the Chicago World's Fair in 1893, and its principles were adopted in the great power installations at Niagara Falls. In 1896 Westinghouse and G.E. entered into a cross-patenting system and they were able to join in prosecuting patent infringements of smaller concerns. Their intra-company competition was in products rather than in prices.

Despite the straightened circumstances which followed the 1893 panic, there were plenty of customers for electrical products. Electric streetcars increased in number from 3,000 in 1890 to 51,000 in 1902. But hardly had the uses of electricity for transportation become generally adopted, when the internal combustion engine entered into competition. The ultimate result was the decline and disappearance of the electric automobile, and later, because of new highways and streets, the motor car supplanted the electric streetcar and interurban railways.

This industrial revolution meant vast changes in the distribution of the population. The nation moved with inexorable speed from a rural agricultural civilization to an urban industrial one. The typical American living on a subsistence farm—the Jeffersonian vision of true democracy—was vanishing. Agriculture was no longer the greatest source of national wealth. Even the nature of the farm itself was changing under the impact of machinery. In 1880 the urban population was 28.2 per cent of the total. In 1900 this percentage rose to 39.7, and in 1920 it passed the 50 per cent mark. By 1960 the farm population fell to 10 per cent.

The political changes which accompanied this shift were decisive and permanent. In the era from the end of the Civil

War to the 1890s, reform agitation was rural and the populists were in revolt against the banks and the railroads. The remedy universally proposed was inflation in various forms. But after 1900 the conflict shifted to another area with new modes of proposed change. This movement, which marked the period from 1900 to the outbreak of the war in Europe in 1914, took the name of Progressivism.

The protest against concentrated industrial and financial power appeared in a vast literature. Theodore Roosevelt called this "muckraking," but his political strategy was based upon taking advantage of the swelling public opinion which resulted from the pioneer protests.

Concentration on land reform and monetary schemes turned to efforts to curb "big business," monopoly, and the alliances between business and political parties. Government intervention gained widespread support.

Organized labor was coming to life. European socialism failed to attract the leaders of the labor movement. But strongly organized bargaining units were the goal of the American Federation of Labor from the time of its creation in 1886. Samuel Gompers and others championed a labor power neither aspiring to be a political party itself nor encumbered by any attachment to an existing party but free to cast its votes for its friends and against its enemies.

. The new and rapidly growing cities provided a fertile ground for the growth of irresponsible and often corrupt political machines. A sort of proletariat appeared whose votes were manageable. The influx of a wave of immigration furthered this development. No inconsiderable part of the literature of protest which was appearing aimed at municipal corruption, waste, crime, and disease.

The tremendous impact of reform had its permanent effect. There were, on the plus side, unmistakable improvements in public and political morality. But like so many wholesome movements, reform too had its excesses. Under nonpartisan legislation the responsibility of parties and the two-party system itself were gravely weakened. And the impulse toward government intervention created a beginning for the problems of super-government and bureaucracy which persist in the current scene.

Chapter VII

NEW EXPLORATIONS
IN ENGINEERING

IN 1913 John C. Lincoln had reached, at forty-seven, what he had reason to believe—considering his excellent health and the longevity of his ancestors—to be the middle span of his life. Forty-six more years of activity were to fulfill this expectation.

His company, from incredibly small beginnings and from time to time beset by harsh vicissitudes, had grown to the stature of a solid and successful national institution. Nineteen-thirteen witnessed several considerations which prompted profoundly important reflections about where he stood, where he wanted to go, what he wanted to do, and what priorities should govern the manner in which he might most usefully and peacefully spend the years stretching ahead. It was a moment for a wholesale choice of careers.

Lincoln realized what would be the manner of life, the essential activities, and the personal denials demanded of the working head of a big corporation. These were, he realized, not congenial to his temperament, character, and sense of values. The rewards offered by such a position were power,

79

publicity, and a wide range of associations and personal contact with others in the same positions. The demands would be heavy obligations—financial problems, customer relations, sales management, and personnel problems, speeches, and public appearances, plus luncheons and dinners without end, law suits, legislative hearings, public and press relations, and mass-production techniques to master. Such exactions on time and energy would, he saw, frustrate and terminate the creative, experimental quest which had even earlier become the light and inspiration of his life.

Such a choice had confronted another creative mind more than a decade earlier—that of Thomas Alva Edison. It had also confronted Charles F. Brush. There had developed out of Edison's many inventions several important corporate enterprises. But early in the 1890s there had appeared out of many mergers and promotions the beginnings of what was to become the giant General Electric Company. A great manager had appeared, Charles A. Coffin, who became head of the company. For a while it was the Edison General Electric Company and later simply General Electric. Edison was enabled to devote his life to his more congenial role in the laboratory.

For a short time Lincoln divided his time between the two activities—the direction of Lincoln Electric and detached experimentation. For the latter purpose he opened a workshop in a modest loft building at 2400 Woodland Avenue. With him went four or five employees of Lincoln Electric as assistants. One was an old associate, Joseph T. Uebbing, who had been a sort of trouble shooter at Lincoln Electric. In this new atmosphere Lincoln spent many hours in experimentation in electrical engineering.

The opportunity to spend more and more time at Woodland Avenue while Lincoln Electric might grow into greatness was provided by the services of Lincoln's brother, James F., who had already revealed remarkable capacities as a manager and salesman. James F. was possessed of all the characteristics of a successful head of a growing company. He was tremendously energetic, articulate, and razor-keen as an executive. The management methods of the Ford company intrigued him, while he had a grasp of the engineering problems involved in the electrical business in which the company was engaged. His presence in the company would assure John C. that Lincoln Electric would not be swallowed up in the giant mergers which were so common at the time and thus that the identity of the business would be preserved. In an interview published thirty years later, John C. remarked: "My brother was better able to push the business at that period than I, and later the success of the company was due to his energy and ability."

Lincoln's life was saddened in 1913 by the death of his wife. Following this loss, he journeyed to Europe. Abroad, the consuming interest of his life—engineering and invention—occupied as much of his time as on the shores of Lake Erie. His recollections of that visit were always of those with whom he had met and exchanged ideas on their common ground. He conferred with several of Europe's foremost engineers.

When he returned he found that, with James F. in sole charge, the affairs of the company had gone well. The relations of the two brothers continued for a time as they had been. They still occupied desks in the same office.

After extended discussions between them, a definitive agreement was reached in early 1914. James F. was to take over the management as vice-president and general manager, with John C. remaining as president. The stock was divided three ways, one third to each of the brothers and the remainder held in reserve for key employees.

The shift in the direction of John C.'s life was somewhat of a wrench, but abundant satisfactions were found in the work at Woodland Avenue. The remarkable productivity of his mind in the years that followed is shown by the fact that in the fourteen years that followed the 1914 reorganization Lincoln was granted no less than twenty patents. Most of these were signed over to the company. For his interest in Lincoln Electric remained keen and productive. Company employees recalled many years later his dropping into the plant from day to day for an hour or so, stopping occasionally to look over a worker's shoulder to note some new angle in production methods and talking with officers and other employees about their problems. As always, he was more concerned with customers' problems than with their money.

Lincoln always found time to give the benefits of his unique skill in solving problems in the plants of the major customers of Lincoln Electric. Uebbing recalls that he saw Lincoln returning from Akron on several successive days with his face red from exposure to the arc at the Akron Selle Company where the company was installing a very large welding machine.

In all the interviews which have been conducted in the preparation of this book, with old associates with whom he worked both before and after 1914, there is testimony of Lincoln's kindness and thoughtfulness. Always, he was patient with their progress, however slow; tolerant of their mistakes. He was always receptive to their suggestions and even criticisms of his ideas and work, prompt to recognize his own mistakes in judgment and quick to change direction whenever that became advisable.

At Woodland Avenue, Lincoln turned seriously to a project which combined his experience with welding with his earlier work with electric railways. In electric railways the current flows through a circuit composed of the overhead wire, the car, and one of the rails beneath. Electricity comes from the wire, down the trolley, through the motor, and back through the rail to the power station. Efficient operation demands continuous and sound connections between the rails. In 1913 Lincoln filed a patent application for connecting rails by using a welding arc to fuse the ends of strips of copper to the rail ends and each joint. After his work at Woodland Avenue began he applied himself to this idea and in so doing worked out several of his later welding developments.

Nineteen-fifteen marked the formation of a new company with John C. Lincoln as president. Since its name, The Lincoln Bonding Company, was suggestive of a financial rather than a manufacturing concern, in 1919 it was rechristened the Rail Welding and Bonding Company. E. R. Alexander was associated with Lincoln in this venture. At first, the company made only the copper bonds and machines for welding these to the rail-ends. But later, when the concept of fusing rail-ends directly together developed, the plant altered production to make possible this more effective and economical type of welding. The first customer was the Boston Electric Railway Company, to be followed over several years—until the early 1920s—by many other systems throughout the country. In 1920 Lincoln dropped out of the rail-welding business. Although the business was sold in 1930, it continued production —long after street railways had given way to the automobile, the bus, and the fast commuter train—by branching out into the wider field of industrial welding, where it remained until 1946.

83

In those happy, creative years at the Woodland Avenue plant Lincoln was in the habit of doing most of his drafting in his home on Terrace Road. There, sitting over his drawing board near the fireplace, in the living room, John C. worked evenings and mornings until about 11 A.M. when he would depart for the Woodland or the Kelley Avenue plant. Aside from reading, drafting was his recreation.

Nearly a half a century later—at the close of his life—the same drawing board occupied a significant place in his Phoenix home. It was more than mere memento of the past, for in late years he had used it in his work on improving the industrial techniques in copper mining. The old board had served Lincoln well since those days so distant in time and space and in the industrial rise of America.

Aside from his attention to Lincoln Electric and the rail-bonding businesses, John C. Lincoln's consuming interest was invention. From 1913 when he opened his experimental shop on Woodland Avenue to 1931 when he left Cleveland to live in Arizona, Lincoln gained twenty-six patents issued by the United States Patent Office. Half of these pertained to welding, applicable not only to the apparatus being developed at Lincoln Electric but to his rail-welding enterprise. The others, for the most part, were related to improvements and developments of his earlier motor and dynamo designs. There was also a patent for meat curing, on which he had taken three earlier patents. Fifty-five patents bore his name, running from his first in 1891 to his last in 1961.*

In 1928 John C. moved up to chairman of the board of Lincoln Electric and James F. became president. In 1931, for reasons related in another chapter, he moved to Phoenix, Arizona,

---

* A list of these patents appears in the Appendix with subjects, dates, and numbers.

where he was to reside the remaining twenty-eight years of his life, with frequent visits to Cleveland where many of his interests were located.

As he left Cleveland, looking back on the thirty-six years since he had established a business of his own, John C. Lincoln could survey a career that spanned a veritable revolution in the application of electricity. From its flickering start electricity had come to be utilized in all industry and, indeed, in the service of practically all mankind. He had in that period, in addition to his remarkable series of inventions, started three business enterprises. Two of them became leaders in their field. He had established associations with several others. He had won the respect and admiration of hundreds of leaders in the life of Cleveland and the nation. He was instrumental in making Cleveland, for a number of those years, first in the electrical industry. When he turned to the West he had earned high rank among its first citizens.

Chapter VIII

AN ART THAT
BECAME AN INDUSTRY

Two desks, standing in the president's office at Lincoln Electric for some years, symbolized a remarkable relationship. Although the desks were only a few feet apart, the two brothers, John C. and James F., saw each other after 1914 only occasionally. John C. seldom used his desk during his frequent visits to the plant, since he was chiefly interested in the machinery of production. Each of the brothers, with inborn drive, followed the course most suited to his individual capacity, vision, and temperament. In the enterprise in which their fortunes were joined continuous personal contacts were quite irrelevant. But to use a symbolic word, there was a welding of talents which produced a homogeneous achievement of massive proportions. There flowed from both a creative current so powerful that the outcome was not only a great industrial enterprise but a revolutionary development that permeated almost every industry in the nation.

Lincoln Electric continued to be a major concern of John C. after his base of operations shifted to Woodland Avenue. This is shown by his assigning the greater part of the inventions developed there to Lincoln Electric. Mainly they were concerned with motor design and new developments in arc welding. Usually they were created in solving problems that arose from the rapidly growing motor business of the company, for until the 1920s that was the main factor in production. But no less than thirteen of his patents in that period related to welding.

As we have seen, arc welding originated in the experiments of a Frenchman in the early 1880s. It remained an interesting trick long before serious industrial application was needed or considered practical. Many minds were attracted by the concept, but a quarter of a century was to elapse before it could be seriously considered as an important factor in industry. As in the case of so many marvelous devices which have enriched American life, such as the motion picture and its lusty progeny television, an art became a scientific fact and later an engineering reality. No individual contributed more toward bringing welding into industrial use than John C. Lincoln.

Two applications for patents, filed in 1918, indicate how astutely Lincoln understood not only the technical problems involved but the industrial potentialities of welding. His language, filed with one of these applications, was not only characteristically plain and direct, but illuminated with a vision of the future:

"My invention related to improvements in method of welding, has for its object the production of a weld which will be ductile, as strong or stronger than the metal welded, economical in the cost of labor and current, and which preferably avoids the preparation of the materials welded.

"Incidentally, my object further contemplates the control of the electric arc by which the welding is accomplished, so that it may be most efficiently directed to the successive points at which the welding takes place, and steadied for the production of a strong, ductile and even weld . . .

"The principal objection to the work hitherto produced . . . is that the welds are lacking in ductility, while another objection is found in that said welds are not as strong as the metal united . . .

"During my experiments I have ascertained that in order to obtain ductility in a weld, it is necessary to avoid as far as possible the oxidizing action of the air, and this I have accomplished by using both an inert gas about the arc, and a protective medium for the weld, which I may term slag . . .

"By employing the method or methods above outlined, riveting may be avoided, and much of the work upon steel bridges, steel hulls for vessels, boilers, and the like may be performed with material gain of time at a very much lower cost than is possible with riveting."

Consider the final sentence above and look around you at the manufacturing world today, forty years later. A sense of the quality of Lincoln's vision is apparent.

Although many others were driving at the same problems, both in Europe and the United States, Lincoln's inventions in this period were to lead to developments toward automatic machine welding—a process which now assumes major importance in mechanized manufacturing. In fact, some of Lincoln's patents, long expired, contain ideas which have illuminated manufacturing ever since. The "inert gas" to which he refers in the application quoted above, used as a shielding agent, was carbon dioxide. Today the automotive industry and others using lighter gauge metals are putting carbon dioxide to use in this way in welding. Lincoln's idea of putting fluxing material on the seam to be welded was a forerunner of the most widely used automatic process, submerged arc welding.

Another patent granted to him was for a tubular rod in which the fluxing materials were sealed. This too has found modern, even universal, application. The use of slag, to which he refers, has become a basic practice in all arc welding. Adding alloys to the weld metal through the flux was recognized by Lincoln as a possibility. He also showed a keen appreciation for controlling the arc and for improving the consistency of the weld quality. Several of his early devices provided means for guiding and directing the electrode rather than leaving it to the operator's dexterity.

Later, in the 1920s, he carried some of these ideas to a logical conclusion. Lincoln patented a self-propelled machine which traveled over the seam and automatically made the weld. He took out several patents for devices to feed the electrode automatically during the welding process and to regulate the length of the arc. Lincoln Electric, always outstanding in dramatizing its products and activities, gave this the colorful name "Electronic Tornado."

John C.'s continuing interest in welding brought him into the activity of the newly-formed American Welding Society. He presented papers at some of its meetings and served on various committees. In 1934 the Society presented him with its highest award, the Samuel Wylie Miller Medal for "Meritorious Achievement." The award cited him for his work on the variable voltage machine, the ductility and strength of welds, the carbon arc automatic process, and his efforts to expand the use of welding in many industries.

Beyond doubt, his imagination and inventions, together with James F.'s genius for management, public relations, and capacity for seeing opportunities for projecting this new device into wider usefulness, firmly established Lincoln Electric as the pioneer and leader in electric arc welding—a position it holds today in a crowded and highly competitive field.

When the First World War threw its shadow over Europe, its impact upon the United States took the form of providing the distracted nations over there with products they were unable to make themselves. Motor orders came in a tide from Britain and other countries. To speed the manufacture of the necessary products, James F. organized a meeting of motor manufacturers in Washington at which he proposed that the entire industry standardize products.

Later in the war, as this country was called upon to speed shipbuilding—to create what had been called "a bridge of ships"—James F. arranged a meeting with some of the Navy's top admirals. He wanted to show how much weight could be saved, how much speed could be increased, and how much more soundness could be built into ships by welding. Pessimism was strong among these officers, not in regard to weight and speed, but strength and seaworthiness in such construction. One admiral remarked that he could "kick off with my foot any weld you can make." James F. replied that the admiral "would have a damned sore toe if he tried."

But welding was to justify all that James F. claimed. In the German rearmament the limitation of tonnage imposed by the Versailles treaty and the Washington Arms Conference later was evaded by welding the hulls of warships. This not only gave their ships more punch for their weights but provided greater capacity to stand punishment. For example, in the 1930s the Germans were able to mount battleship armament on their cruiser-class ships and incorporate unexcelled compartmentation into their hulls. Other nations followed this example. When the Second World War demanded an immense supply of shipping, welding became standard practice with results that stand as an incredible feat of fast production.

Despite the basic inventions and methods of production, several years were to pass in which welding machinery remained a minor factor in the business of Lincoln Electric. In 1920 the company was producing about seventy welders a month. The bulk of its business was in motors until 1922, when welders became more important. At that time welding was used mainly for repairing castings, railroad equipment, drums, tanks, fans, and blowers.

Other companies negotiated for licenses under Lincoln patents. The company's policy was not to restrict the use of its processes by other companies. It realized that the more companies worked to reduce costs, the more welding would become universally used in all industry. Lincoln Electric began an extensive publicity campaign to popularize welding. Ultimately, all machinery, except for a few machine tools, was made with welded construction.

The prosperity of Lincoln Electric has not been based upon a monopoly position, but rather upon a number of complementary factors—an initial lead and advantage in building certain types of motors, concentration on finding lower-cost methods, the wise use of engineering talent, the good will that the company has established in the industrial world, and teamwork in the company itself largely through its famous profit-sharing plan devised by James F. Lincoln.

Though a strong individualist himself, James F. has always placed great stress upon teamwork within the company. Shortly after he became vice president and general manager in 1914, he set up an advisory board composed of elected representatives from all departments of the company. This board has met regularly twice a week ever since. It serves as a two-way channel of information and ideas between management and workers. Out of its discussions, and vigorously pushed by James F., there was developed the system of "incentive management." Basic in the policies developed were the piecework system, cost of living multiplier in wage determination, bonuses, paid vacations, insurance, employee stock ownership and merit rating.

Notable top management people have been recruited and developed over the years. Joseph Merriam joined the company in 1914 as secretary and later assumed charge of the credit department. In 1916 C. M. Taylor, educated at Western Reserve University, was recruited. After service as a pilot in the First World War, he became factory superintendent and was responsible for many of the company's cost-reducing processes. In 1920 George Landis, a brilliant young engineer who had worked at Westinghouse, joined the company. He developed many refinements in welding and became engineering vice-president.

A most notable figure in the company's history was A. F. "Charlie" Davis who after graduation from Ohio State was recommended to James F. by its engineering department. He was employed and after a brief tour of the plant was sent to the Chicago sales office. In 1928 he became vice-president. His great contribution was in developing educational and promotional activities. He wrote extensively for publication and his book on welding is a standard text.

From Cologne, Germany, came William Irrgang, who was to become engineering vice-president. His genius in electrical engineering produced new and revolutionary methods in manufacturing electrodes, cutting costs of production by one half. In 1951 he became president of the company and James F. assumed the chairmanship of the board.

With ship welding well established here at the beginning of the Second World War, the demand for electrodes grew and the government asked Lincoln Electric to increase its production in that line. James F. rejected the government's offer to build an additional plant and undertook to meet the demand for electrodes by showing his competitors how to speed their production with the methods Irrgang and others had developed.

Training people in the plant to understand welding and to operate welding machinery has been a company project for more than forty years. In that period it has trained 50,000 people.

But this training has been only one phase of its educational effort. Before the company could sell welders, it had to sell welding as an industrial necessity. The company's policy held that if enough companies could be persuaded that with welding they could improve and reduce the cost of their products, Lincoln Electric would get its share of the new business thus created. Hence its public relations program has always been stressed. It publishes a magazine called *The Stabilizer*, named after one of John C.'s inventions, texts and handbooks, engineering information, teaching aids such as films and slides, and technical articles in journals and newspapers. It has conducted prize essay competitions on welding. Its advertising took on the character of educational material. For some years it ran a campaign that became famous as the "Pop and Lad" series, Pop representing tradition and Lad in the role of a questioning youth. Throughout the public statements, addresses, and other public utterances, James F. preached the fundamental American principles of self-help so characteristic of the principles of both Lincoln brothers.

Dramatic devices were used to draw attention to the com-

93

pany's products. For years a motor submerged in water was on exhibition in the company lobby to show the capacity of the product to operate under novel circumstances.

The motor expansion during the First World War and the rapid expansion of welding in all industry demanded additional plant space. In 1922 the Grant Motor Car Company with a big plant at 12718 Coit Road, on the eastern edge of Cleveland, liquidated its business, and, while the space looked overly large at the time, Lincoln Electric took it and moved from Kelley Avenue. This plant, with several additions which almost doubled its floor area, sufficed until after the Second World War. In 1951 a new modern plant was built on St. Clair Avenue in Euclid, an eastern suburb of Cleveland. It has thirty acres of floor space with approximately 1,200 employees and had a gross business in 1960 of $58,705,000. Lincoln Electric's motor business was temporarily discontinued during the Second World War, but after 1945 this was resumed along with some battery charger production.

In 1936 a notable resolution was passed by the board on motion by John C. Lincoln, chairman, which signalized its abiding faith in the further development of welding:

"Since the dawn of recorded time, man has struggled constantly to improve his conditions. Coping with many obstacles, he has developed great skill and ingenuity. Applied through the years, these talents have rewarded men with luxuries of which his ancestors never dreamed—the telephone, the radio, the automobile, the airplane, the railroad, the steamship, the skyscraper, the gigantic bridge—these modern wonders and many others are the products of man's skill and ingenuity.

"Recent years have seen the origin and development of an ingenious process which has had great economic, social and

94

commercial significance to mankind. That process is arc welding.

"It is, therefore, our belief that by encouraging and stimulating scientific interest in and study of welding, still greater benefits will result from man's skill and ingenuity. To this end, The Lincoln Electric Company announces that it has created, in honor of its President, 'The James F. Lincoln Arc Welding Foundation.'"

This foundation concerns itself with education in the field of arc welding, distributing books on the subject and sponsoring contests in schools.

Prelude to Chapter IX

FOLLOWING its impressive performance in the First World War the American economy, after a brief hesitation, moved to unprecedented levels. From 1921 to 1929 our national income increased nearly 40 per cent. Our gross national product moved upward from $69 billion to $104 billion. By 1928 Herbert Hoover, as a candidate for President, was justified in asserting that American capitalism had justified itself. There seemed assured a production level to meet the needs of all and to reduce poverty to a satisfactory minimum.

But as the boom of the 1920s proceeded, a certain number of underlying weaknesses and dangers appeared to perceptive observers. Expansion had involved a vast credit structure accompanied by widespread borrowing from savings. Speculation grew alarmingly, at first in land in Florida and then in the stock market. Individual enterprises and state and local governments leaped headlong into debt. Machines and plants, roads and schools, automobiles, homes, and household accessories were financed by borrowing. The vanishing illusions of winning the war and the assurance of perpetual peace were replaced by new illusions.

Symptoms of economic distress had appeared here and there under the flush of health. Farmers, who had overextended to meet the food shortages of war, were in trouble throughout the 1920s. Their market was shrinking, and their prices declined. As surpluses grew, shipping rusted at American docks. A declining level of construction persisted after 1925.

On October 29, 1929 there came a crisis in the stock market. Sixteen million shares were dumped in one day in the New York Stock Exchange. Later a wave of panic swept the nation, submerging businesses, banks, and railroads. Factory doors closed upon wage workers, clerks, engineers, and executives. Unemployment rose to new high levels.

Although President Hoover's administration offered encouraging bulletins and important businessmen assured the public that we were witnessing only a summer storm, the statistics belied such optimism. The durable goods index fell from 110 in 1929 to 58 in 1932. Gross national product declined from 104 to 75, the 1920 level.

President Hoover was not a man to stand aside, untouched by loss, poverty, and personal distress. He labored indefatigably in meetings of businessmen and others to devise ways of stemming the decline. But in 1930 the Democrats won the House of Representatives, and, as is always the way of politics, the new Democratic leadership immediately began planning for the election in 1932. Hoover, however, secured from Congress the enactment of legislation creating the Reconstruction Finance Corporation and the Home Owners Loan Corporation. The RFC, as was later proved, was a brilliant concept of bringing the strong arm of Federal credit to the support of shaky corporations. The HOLC helped to stem the tide of foreclosures.

Nevertheless, a hostile Congress and a population whose

confidence had been shattered by the dissipation of a dream frustrated most of the President's efforts.

Franklin D. Roosevelt, who had been re-elected Governor of New York in 1930 by a tremendous majority, won the Presidential nomination in 1932, and the campaign which followed was almost exclusively devoted to a debate on economic issues. Roosevelt and Hoover disagreed sharply on the causes of the depression. Hoover held that the depression was rooted in foreign dislocations which had reacted upon the economy of the United States. Roosevelt held that our ills stemmed from domestic causes which the Hoover Administration and, before that, the Coolidge Administration had failed to foresee. Some of these, according to Roosevelt, were the excesses of the Hawley-Smoot tariff, the neglect of agriculture, the selling of shaky securities, especially in the public utilities, and losses in foreign investments through the banks and investment houses. He claimed that the first steps toward recovery must be taken at home.

The result in the election followed a pattern which had become traditional in American politics. The electorate, depressed and frustrated by economic problems which were mysteries to most and controversial to some, visited its rebuke upon the political regime in power. Roosevelt exuded charm and confidence. He promised action and outlined certain specifications of the forms which such action would take. Voters turned to the side which promised something new and different. The mandate given the new Administration was clear, although the exact specifications of change were indistinct. About all that a distressed public wanted was change of some sort—any change, as long as it was change.

Traditionally, the election of a new President, even a change in party control, had meant little alteration in the character of the economic system. With occasional alterations in tariffs and monetary policy, the economic system went on as usual, with its inevitable ups and downs in the level of prosperity and enterprise.

But for a number of reasons this change in political control was destined to mark a sharp divergence from the past. One reason was the severe shaking of public confidence in the efficacy of old economic laws of supply and demand to maintain a stable economy. Another was the mobilization in the new Administration of the remnants of many of the reformers and reform movements of the preceding generation. Finally, there was the character and temperament of the new President. Roosevelt was an activist, curious, experimental, daring, and almost entirely lacking in any fixed philosophy of economics and constitutional policy.

Gathered under his leadership were old populists who believed the key to progress and universal well-being lay in manipulation of the money supply, devoted advocates of a more stringent exercise by government of regulatory power over economic affairs, and also a younger group of reformers who were intrigued by the idea of national economic planning —a type of over-all planning which took shape in the management of European economies in the First World War and which was adopted wholesale by Lenin in the early days of the Soviet regime in Russia. There were also socialistic elements whose concern was in the public ownership of the production and transmission of electric power.

All of these somewhat discordant elements were made a

part of the new order. There was little discrimination among them by Roosevelt. Later, as we shall see, he added another element to the mixture, the concept that the volume and nature of the national product could be governed by spending public revenues for various sorts of public works.

But on one point Roosevelt's purpose was perfectly clear. He believed in enlarging the Federal establishment and its power in line with the New Nationalism preached but never put into effect by Theodore Roosevelt two decades before.

From 1933 to 1935, however, Roosevelt's moves were not especially unorthodox. There was a vital necessity to provide personal relief for the needy and for raising the prices of what agriculture produced. In fact, his first two moves were completely orthodox. The banks, which had reached a state of almost complete collapse when he entered office, were saved by Federal measures which proved to be effective. Also, he introduced economy measures which cut Federal expenses drastically.

He abandoned gold and labored to raise prices to a level which predated the onset of the depression by three years. In those early years he adopted policies which foreclosed greater international intercourse. While there was talk about changing tariff rates, little was done in that traditional means of stimulating the economy.

Nevertheless, Roosevelt secured the creation of the Tennessee Valley Authority, which was a radical first step toward projecting the Federal government into the business of producing and distributing electric power. And through the Securities and Exchange Act he provided through the Federal government a means of protecting investors.

All the measures adopted in those early years of the Roosevelt Administration came to be known as the New Deal, although they represented no consistent pattern of policy, except that they were designed to project the power and authority of the Federal government into services and activities hitherto left to state and local governments and also to private initiative and enterprise.

The effect of these measures upon the economy will be debated for generations to come. There was an unmistakable rise in the well-being of farmers, a considerable rise in the volume and variety of manufacturing, a lessening of personal distress, and a fairly prudent management of the finances of the Federal government, although it would be many years before deficits were eliminated.

Employment increased slowly, and international trade made appreciable gains.

The gross national product increased substantially, from $58 billion in 1932 to $82 billion in 1936.

In certain lines, however, new technology made for notable increases. The production of electric power increased spectacularly and, with it, manufacturing in electrical equipment.

The Lincoln Electric Company survived the depression in excellent condition. In part this was due to the inherent soundness of its products and the efficiency of its management.

But the heavy industries were not greatly affected until the coming of war production in 1940.

Chapter IX

THE SENIOR CITIZEN GOES WEST

THE long life of John C. Lincoln falls into three periods. There were the twenty-nine years before the founding of the Lincoln Electric Company in 1895. Thirty-six years followed before he visited Arizona in 1931. Then a kind Providence gave him twenty-eight more years. Those last years, past the customary retirement age of sixty-five, proved to be the most varied, interesting, and profitable of all.

The premise behind the outmoded customs of retirement at sixty-five is that the people who are now politely called "senior citizens" are to be unproductive and unprofitable—a private burden and a public problem. Less than a century ago Emerson wrote, when he reached an age when John C. Lincoln was still at his best:

> 'Tis time to be old
> To take in sail . . .
> There's not enough for this and that.

No such suggestion of a life at checkers and shuffleboard could conceivably have appeared in Lincoln's mind. He had plans, unfinished business in welding techniques, social and economic ideals to further, a zestful interest in the possibilities of the new country he was exploring, material means to invest in productive enterprise, and the undiminished vigor of perfect health.

Nature, character, and inheritance had given him the expectancy of many years of life. His habits had been temperate. He had needed little medical attention. And his insatiable curiosity and drive were in themselves life-giving.

The life of the Lincoln family had been a happy one. Lincoln enjoyed being close to his family while he worked.

His first wife, Myrtie Virginia Humphrey, whom he had married in Columbus in 1891, died in 1913. There were two children born of this marriage, Myrtie Louise (Mrs. Peter Kerr), and John Gladden.

In 1914 he married Mary Dearstyne Mackenzie (called Meride) in Pittsfield, Massachusetts. She died in 1917. Her friend, Helen Colvill, became acquainted with Lincoln after the death of Meride, and they were married in 1918.

Helen had been a high-school teacher in Circleville, Ohio. Her cultural interests were wholesome and varied, and, above all, she had a keen, practical mind. These attributes proved to be invaluable in their association during the forty-one years that followed. Three children were born—Lillian Colvill in 1921, Joseph Colvill in 1922, and David Colvill in 1925.

In the years before 1931 the Lincoln family had lived in the Cleveland area, where they had a home in East Cleveland and another in the country at Aurora, Ohio.

In 1931 the great depression hung over the United States and much of the Western World. But Lincoln's business interests were safe. Lincoln Electric, capably managed and busy exploring the great potentialities of welding, was weathering the storm without trouble. Lincoln's further exploration of the techniques of welding could be carried on wherever he was located.

For the most part, the reason for a decision to spend the winter of 1931–32 in Arizona was the health of Mrs. Lincoln and Lillian. It was clear that a milder climate would be profitable for both.

Lincoln's interest in electrical manufacturing had given him a comprehensive knowledge of metallurgy and had taken him to New Mexico in 1913 in search of mica, a material used in armature manufacturing and which is useful because it is an excellent insulator. While prospecting there—he recalled later —he had lived on goat's milk and bread and had grown to appreciate the value of that diet. It served him well in critical times in his later life.

The Lincolns arrived in Phoenix in December 1931, and planned to return to Ohio in April. They had no thought of living permanently in Arizona and so they took quarters at the Jokake Inn, a notable tourist spot near the Camelback Mountain. There was already some evidence of the growth of Phoenix toward Scottsdale near Camelback Mountain.

Lincoln's winter was filled with activity. His major concern was the final development of welding techniques for Lincoln Electric, but he had time also to survey the new West in which he found himself and to realize that, beyond the depression which prevailed over the nation, this desert area was full of attractive possibilities.

Thus occupied, he had little time to enter into the social activities of the Jokake Inn. Nor was he much concerned about the impression he was making on the fashionable winter guests who were there. To them, the Lincolns were at first just another Midwestern farm family of moderate means whose eccentric father spent much time puttering about with strange mechanical devices. (He carried on his experimentation on a ductile weld in a small room with a spare bathtub.)

Meanwhile, the spell of Arizona, so full of reminders of wild western life, gripped the Lincoln imagination. Here, where he was living, he could see the possibilities for growth through the building of winter residences, industries suitable to the limitations of the climate, and what the chambers of commerce call "tourism."

The land was cheap, and, before Lincoln left in the spring, he had purchased a considerable area of land, mostly for the payment of delinquent taxes and amounting to about $20 an acre, at the foot of Mummy Mountain. This area, near Camelback Mountain, is now a large part of what is called Paradise Valley. That name hardly applied to the landscape then. It was stark desert, relieved only by giant cactus, brush, and rocks. In the final weeks of their stay in 1932, the Lincolns decided to return in the fall.

But not to Jokake Inn. Instead, they rented a house at what is now Camelback Road and 32nd Street. Lincoln set up his workshop in the laundry room. The children were entered in the desert schools.

"Even when Daddy was at his busiest," said Mrs. Lincoln of that period, "he always had time for the children. Every afternoon at five—it was almost a ritual—he would take them for a long walk before dinner. No doubt with the austere life he had been compelled to live as a child in his mind, he sought to make his children's days pleasant and free. He never lectured or scolded them. He expected them to do right and they almost always did."

In the spring of 1933, while the nation watched the swiftly moving activities of the New Deal in Washington, the Lincoln family returned to Cleveland. That summer they broke their stay in Ohio with a few weeks' stay at Chautauqua, New York. Chautauqua had always been a favorite spot for a summer's visit. Lincoln and Mrs. Lincoln had been there for short periods. From 1933 on they made almost annual trips there for a number of days, attending the lectures and concerts. When they returned to Arizona that fall, they rented another house on Camelback Road and Lincoln arranged with Carl H. Schelin for work space in his Valley Machine Shop in downtown Phoenix.

His twelve years' labor on the perfection of the ductile weld was nearing success. Before Lincoln's discoveries, a weld made with an electric arc was as brittle as cast iron. Lincoln realized that only by some method of excluding air from the welding operation could oxidization be prevented and a bendable weld be achieved. This, he believed, could be accomplished only through the composition and handling of the fluxing material. Gradually he succeeded in creating the right composition of the flux and its treatment under the electric arc. He found that the materials in the flux take up the oxygen faster than the metals to be joined. The result was a patentable flux which made the weld as flexible as steel.

The patent on the ductile weld was only one of the many which he registered between 1931 and 1956. Most of the work on these was done in Arizona.

In 1934 the Lincolns decided to make their permanent home in Arizona, and they purchased a house in the same locality in which they had lived in the three years before. Here Lincoln established his workshop in a two-car garage.

He had come to the conclusion that Arizona had two assets which were destined to contribute to making the desert state an important part of the nation. One was its mineral resources. The other, its climate, would bring many tourists and winter residents. Accordingly Lincoln turned his attention to the developing of these assets.

His property in Paradise Valley now amounted to 320 acres. With the exception of the spot on which his newly acquired home was located, this land was destitute of human habitation. But with recovery from the depression, there developed a considerable interest in the possibilities of the Phoenix area and land prices increased.

But full development of the area could only come, he realized, if enough people of substance who might become interested in the region's singular natural advantages could be attracted for short winter sojourns.

Lincoln found the answer in the dreams and plans of a man who had come to the Phoenix area a few years before. He was Jack Stewart, whose ambition was to become the manager of a first-class resort hotel. Stewart was a native of North Dakota who had been engaged in public relations before coming to Arizona. When Lincoln met him, he was manager of The Wigwam, a hotel with cottages in Litchfield Park, an enterprise of the Goodyear Tire and Rubber Company. At a time when Goodyear had been a major consumer of cotton, it had acquired large areas of land near Phoenix for its production. The Wigwam had been built to house visiting executives of the company. Later it accepted other guests.

Stewart was a competent manager, but he wanted to be the proprietor of an inn which conformed to his ideas of what such an institution should be. A year before he met Lincoln, he had selected the name "Camelback Inn" and decided that because of the success of the Jokake Inn the location should be near the mountain. He discussed his ideas with E. Loomis Bowes, a professional photographer who had moved to Arizona because of his wife's health. Bowes was not a professional architect, but had deep feeling for the beauties of the area and for the deep imprint upon the Southwest made by the Indians and the Spanish. Stewart and Bowes drew up preliminary plans, and these were shown to several people in Phoenix who might have the means to help. Stewart himself had only $5,000.

When Stewart met Lincoln, they found a great deal in common. Lincoln saw the possibility of such an inn as a way to attract people of means to the area, and he had the land which would be an ideal location. Together with Bowes, Lincoln and Stewart selected the exact location, worked out the plans, and arranged the financial details. The Inn was built on a spot where earlier the Lincolns had enjoyed family picnics.

A company was incorporated to which Lincoln sold 300 acres of his land and received stock in payment. Stewart also received stock which would be compensation for supervising the building and later managing the Inn.

Bowes says that, in designing Camelback Inn and its environs, he adhered to no specific type of architecture. Rather, the plans called for a mingling of Hopi, Spanish, and certain original conceptions which were suitable to the natural site and background. The thousands of guests who have visited it since its opening in 1936 can testify to the Inn's unique character. It is "rich but not gaudy"; its quiet beauty invites informality and restfulness. The Inn and the cottages, which are an integral part, occupy a site of 25 acres facing Camelback Mountain. Giant cacti abound, and there are now many orange and grapefruit trees, as well as palms.

The success of the Inn was assured from the start. Guests return, some for a long succession of years. In the beginning there was space for seventy-seven guests, but there have been many enlargements since. The Inn gave considerable acreage to the Paradise Valley Country Club for a golf course to which guests have access.

Lincoln contributed the cash necessary to the initial construction, and later additions have been possible from the profits. The Lincoln interests own forty-five per cent of the stock, and Stewart holds the rest. Lincoln's home in his later years was near the Inn.

Lincoln's first ventures in mining were not so immediately successful, but he gained experience which proved invaluable when later he acquired the Bagdad Copper properties. In 1933 he became interested in the possibility of opening an old gold mine called "The Alaska" near Salome, just west of Wickenburg on the highway to Los Angeles. A humorist named Dick Wick Hall gave Salome some colorful publicity some years ago in *The Saturday Evening Post*. After some investigation Lincoln decided to abandon the venture. Salome is now a town of about two hundred inhabitants. But because of the rumors of a rise in the price of gold, the mine was reopened in 1961.

Next he turned to a much more interesting venture, the old Vulture mine near Wickenburg. The records show that from 1863 to 1887, despite constant harassment from Indians, the Vulture mine produced some $21,000,000 in gold, silver, and lead. An Arizona governor once referred to Vulture in his annual message as "the Comstock of Arizona."

The mine had been operated by an Arizona pioneer, Harry Wickenburg. But in 1887 the main ore vein was lost because of a geological fault. Then disaster after disaster overtook the town that bore Wickenburg's name. A dam was washed away with a loss of eighty lives. This flood also destroyed Wickenburg's ranch. The tired old pioneer after that lived on in the neighborhood and then took his own life at the age of eighty-eight.

In 1907 a new company took over Vulture and sought and found the missing vein. It was operated for another ten years, but again, because of a fault, the operation ended.

The mystery of the vanishing vein challenged Lincoln's lively imagination, and in 1937 he and a mining man named Ernest Dickie acquired a lease on the old mine. They loaded the ore into trucks and carried it to a mill which they had constructed in the vicinity. In 1942 they had reached a gross production of $134,360. But the war regulations overtook them, and priorities for equipment were restricted. Costs were high, and, without new equipment, the mine lost most of what it had gained. Lincoln had three gold buttons placed in a brooch which he presented to Mrs. Lincoln. That, he declared, was the total profit from the venture. The mine was abandoned. But the lost vein of gold is believed by many to remain, a puzzling mystery and a temptation to the venturesome.

Undaunted by these unsuccessful ventures in gold mining, Lincoln moved into a much more ambitious and challenging project. He acquired the Bagdad Copper Corporation in western Arizona. There his bold imagination and engineering skill were at full flood at the age of seventy-eight.

During the years before the Second World War Lincoln had made large investments in real estate and buildings in many parts of the nation. His income was ample; the depression had brought down prices, and his faith in full recovery was firm. In 1944 he bought 2,400 acres of desert land near Higley which is southeast of Phoenix. The land had belonged to the Phelps-Dodge mining interests. They were interested in it only because its allocation of water from the Salt River irrigation project could be useful in its mining operations in the neighborhood. But the Salt River Water Users Association ruled that such a diversion of water from land use could not be permitted. Thus the property was of no use to Phelps-Dodge, and Lincoln acquired it for $350,000. This was very profitable in agricultural projects in the remaining war years. This property has since been sold.

Lincoln also acquired 70 acres of citrus land near Mesa, east of Phoenix. In 1954 he and Mrs. Lincoln bought a 2,000-acre ranch with 197,000 acres of range land rights in Yuma County near the California border. This has been sold since Lincoln's death.

With few exceptions, Lincoln's investments in real property have been successful. But the rise in the value of his land near Camelback Mountain has been sensational. Lincoln himself is authority for the statement that some hundreds of acres acquired there during the 1930s for not more than $20 an acre rose in selling price to more than $10,000 an acre.

The story of Lincoln's life and philosophy indicates that he was never interested in the acquisition of money as an end. Certainly he can hardly be classed as a land speculator. But while studying land values and the circumstances which affected them, he proved to himself the validity of ideas of the man who, next to Christ, had the greatest influence on his life: Henry George. His increment of profit from land came because society added new value. He believed that such profits were not morally justified. And he proved his faith by bestowing a very large part of his fortune on a foundation dedicated to education in land value taxation and the preservation of the free enterprise system.

Chapter X

THE UNIVERSAL
WIRE SPRING COMPANY

I F YOU ARE one of many Americans who has had a drive in
a General Motors automobile in recent years, John C. Lincoln's versatile talent contributed a good deal to your comfort.
For seats in all GM passenger cars—Chevrolet, Buick, Oldsmobile, Pontiac, and Cadillac—utilize a unique spring arrangement
produced by machines of a company that owes its foundation,
survival, and success in large part to John C. Lincoln.

The story of how Lincoln became involved in the business
of developing and producing what is generally referred to as
the corrugated or zigzag spring goes back to late 1937. John
Lincoln was enjoying one of his periodic visits to Cleveland
when he became interested in the labors of a man by the name
of Jacob Kronheim whose shop was situated in one of Lincoln's rental properties. The activity being carried on by
Kronheim had to do with the bending of wire into a zigzag
shape, thereby creating an unusual type of spring. The concept originated in Germany, but Kronheim had made certain
modifications. No machine had been evolved to turn out this
spring effectively and in volume. But Kronheim hoped that

somehow he could devise a way of producing zigzag springs for the furniture industry.

Lincoln recognized the merit of the idea, sensed in his gifted way the practicability and potential of such an innovation, and within a very short time backed his feelings by investing both his energy and money in the undertaking.

It is noteworthy that John C. Lincoln was in his seventy-first year at a time when the country still felt the effects of the depression and those comfortably situated hesitated to shift their weight in business, let alone move out on the slippery deck of enterprise. Few men are given an irrepressible zest for new ventures, particularly with such hazardous going at hand. Sometimes present in youth, it is seldom found in the afternoon of life.

Yet to take on new risks, new challenges, and always the possibility of heavy loss or failure neither frightened John Lincoln nor suppressed his indominable curiosity, his unusual confidence, or his quest to bring about change and improvement.

In early 1938 Lincoln and Kronheim organized the Kinko Spring Company with the aim of developing and marketing furniture seating. Shortly thereafter the name was changed to The Universal Wire Spring Company.

Kronheim felt that Lincoln should meet another man who had become intrigued with the new spring idea some time before and whose enthusiasm had brought him to Cleveland on Sundays to work with Kronheim's people on possible application of the spring to automobiles. This man was Harold Neely, an automotive engineer with seventeen years' experience at the Graham Motor Car Company. At first, Neely had no intention of getting into the business of zigzag springs. However, it was not long before he became convinced that there might be a future for them in automotive manufacturing. Furthermore, it was clear that the day of the independent in the automobile business was ending. The progress charts of the independent were not a source of encouragement; its life expectancy was critically short. Those who could bring themselves to face the unhappy truth were wise to look about for some new occupation.

After Neely recognized that automobile seats as well as furniture might accommodate such springs, he checked with Kronheim and others and found that the way was open, from a patent standpoint, to market a finished product if machines could be developed to turn them out.

Neely's meeting with Lincoln was set for late March. Anticipating the date and feeling that something concrete might better demonstrate automotive application, Neely went to work putting together a small-scale unit constructed from copper tubing, copper sheets, and solder and arranged to appear as much like an upholstered automobile front seat as possible.

"Armed with this material and a lot of enthusiasm for what I thought could be accomplished under the right conditions, I met Mr. Lincoln in Cleveland," Neely recalled some years later. The meeting was productive. Lincoln was impressed. And it was agreed that Neely was to undertake the direction of both the automotive and furniture spring development.

In the corner of a Cleveland tool shop with a small work force, Lincoln and Neely commenced construction of full-sized front-seat structures. By examining, changing, "feeling our way," as Neely put it, they set their sights on a seat they could put into an automobile for further evaluating, testing, and revising. At the same time they contributed to Kronheim's work of exploring and improving the zigzag steel fabric for furniture application.

Among early considerations, Lincoln felt that, if the automotive venture should prove successful, an arrangement should be made with a corporation capable of meeting the tremendous expenditures that would be required to produce in great volume. The Stewart-Warner Corporation showed keen interest, but after several weeks of intensive study, of displaying the samples to a host of engineers in the important automotive companies, and a useless search among known spring machine manufacturers to find a ready method for making the type of spring required, its executives decided they could not participate.

It was Harold Neely's responsibility, when he returned from the disappointing negotiations with Stewart-Warner, to bring Lincoln up to date. John C. had just returned from Phoenix to spend several summer months, living at Mentor with his family. Neely unfolded all the details of the Stewart-Warner situation and the conclusions they had reached. Lincoln listened attentively, then responded without any show of disappointment.

"I think they're absolutely right," he observed. "Unless we have a machine to produce this fabric, we haven't much basis for talking with anybody who is planning to do anything. Why don't we get busy and make a machine?"

To those concerned this was quite a statement. To build a machine capable of producing the zigzag steel fabric at the rate or in a manner that would be suitable seemed a very ambitious task. Lincoln in his quiet way must, even at that moment, have focused his masterful engineering intellect on the sizable project at hand. He returned to his home in Mentor with the earlier plans and faced the problem alone. That problem was

John C. Lincoln at four.

The Reverend
William Elleby
Lincoln and Louisa
Lincoln with their
sons John C. and Paul.

At eighteen after graduating from the
Painesville High School.

RIGHT: In 1891 Lincoln had finished his apprenticeship with Charles F. Brush.

BOTTOM: Lincoln built this electric automobile and initiated the manufacture of equipment for recharging batteries for such vehicles.

The shop and work force of Lincoln Electric in 1900.

RIGHT: The first company-owned Lincoln Electric Plant on Kelley Avenue, Cleveland.

CENTER: The present Lincoln Electric Plant.

LEFT: An early welding machine used in welding automobile frames.

Five John Lincolns in 1958 representing four generations.

his is a 1961 model
the Lincoln weld-
g machine.

The open-pit mining operation at Bagdad.

Lincoln with Senator
Barry Goldwater,
a few days before
Lincoln's death.

Receiving an
honorary degree at
Arizona State College.

Lincoln at ninety
with his grandson
Lincoln Howell.

Lincoln and Jack Stewart planned and built the Camelback Inn near Pho
Photograph by Bowerman—Camelback Inn.

Lincoln Memorial
Chapel at Camelback
Inn. *Photograph by
Bowerman—
Camelback Inn.*

to devise a machine which would produce in quantity a corrugated or zigzag type of metal fabric. Such a machine would have to take a length of spring wire, bend it back and forth into a ribbon approximately two inches wide, and, producing continuously, cut it into precise lengths.

The earlier plans were capable but would require sixteen separate operations. To make it commercially usable, Lincoln felt that this number would have to be reduced to as nearly one operation as possible. He worked the remainder of the summer on the problem and finally reduced the number of operations to three. He then handed his plan to Neely for criticisms and further developments.

As we shall see, Lincoln planned and constructed the models of later machines in Phoenix and then sent them to Cleveland.

Neely laid out the drawings for the early machine, detailed individual parts, added control items to make the wire behave, completed the planning, and proceeded to build a working model. By December 15th, when John C. Lincoln returned, there was a completed machine which could be turned by hand and which produced a zigzag fabric in the form desired.

John C. Lincoln was delighted with the result and generous in praising the Neely modifications which included stripping mechanisms that disengaged the bent wire from the drum and cranks. So satisfactory was this prototype that everyone in the small company felt the invigorating confidence that they had the principles mastered and a mechanism created that could take them closer to quantity production. Immediately, work commenced on a production model.

By coincidence, a designer and inventor of wide experience and ability in the machine-design field—S. G. Blumensaadt— had just completed work on a project in the same tool shop. There he had shown profound interest in the construction of

Universal's new machine. Harold Neely brought about a meeting between Blumensaadt and Lincoln. If the company was to have as big a machine program as would be required to accomplish the production envisioned, a product development program would be essential. Lincoln recognized, as Neely had, the important contributions of which Blumensaadt was capable, and an arrangement was made whereby Blumensaadt joined Universal.

And so the prospects were bright as the company entered the new year of 1939. With the nucleus of an organization, a machine designed to produce the basic steel fabric, and confidence that markets could be found, Universal's executives began to expand the organization in a modest way, remembering that all that had been done and probably all that would be done during the ensuing year involved outgoing expense with no incoming revenues.

Theirs was an unusually harmonious and mutually rewarding arrangement. Lincoln's many responsibilities, particularly his Arizona ventures, denied him the gratification of sharing many of the activities of the new organization. The problems of the growing company, including the development of an automotive market, fell most heavily upon his two outstanding associates—Neely, who headed Universal as president, and Blumensaadt, who directed machine building. Both were inspired by the confidence Lincoln displayed. The steadfastness of his financial backing in the long, touch-and-go years before profits showed on the books was a characteristic of Lincoln that had impressed many observers before.

By May of 1939 two improved machines were performing successfully, capable of turning out various gauges of wire into the continuous material and with a new cutting device separating it into desired lengths.

Neely spent considerable time making contacts with engineers in automotive companies. It was a gratifying day when officers of Willys-Overland Motors of Toledo, who had been following Universal's progress, came through with an arrangement for a front seat for the small passenger car they were building. This was appealing because Willys-Overland was building in small volume. By August 1939 production lines had been set up in a plant on East 69th Street, acquired the previous January. A pilot run proved acceptable in mid-August and Universal's production reached about 200 units a day. The following year Willys-Overland decided to use Universal's spring construction in the rear seat of their cars, and in July 1941 an order was placed for a rear-seat, back spring construction for their principal volume models. During 1940 and 1941 there was encouraging experimental work with the engineering staff of General Motors Corporation, which financed exhaustive tests. These studies had reached a point where a decision was imminent when war broke over the United States. Operations on automobile production were discontinued in January 1942.

Paralleling the automotive activity there had been development of furniture applications which required a complete tooling setup. Kronheim had endeavored to interest furniture manufacturers in the corrugated spring systems, and in the face of general resistance to a simplified spring assembly had realized some success. But it was not enough, and clearly only a greater effort in the automotive line could offset the expense of what had really been, up to this time, largely a development phase in Universal's operations.

As the nation plunged into war the Universal Wire Spring Company faced a critical situation. Years later, Harold Neely vividly remembered the uncertainty of the moment: "This could have been the end of Universal. We had not been able to put any meat on our bones. Mr. Lincoln could very well have said, 'Well, I've brought it this far. Where do we fit into the war effort? We're not prepared to make anything except a few wrinkled up pieces of spring wire, so we'd better just wash it up and call it a day.' "

But looking back over the years, Neely marveled that he had never seen John Lincon's confidence waver, never heard a faltering or discouraging sentence uttered by the man. Things would turn out. The future would justify the present. A way would be found to succeed.

While the unnatural appetite of war destroyed certain lines of production and certain enterprises, its satisfaction required enormous outpourings in other lines. It created new enterprises and, in many instances, smaller companies with resourcefulness sufficient to shift their operations to meet particular needs of the moment. To a degree never imagined, a nation's armed strength obtained astonishing mobility. On the world's oceans our ships and boats transported millions of men, their weapons and equipment and their logistic support. Our aircraft, in unprecedented numbers, flew to or over every embattled part of the globe. On the world's land masses the American fighting man and many of his allies relied upon American vehicles. One was destined for fame—the Jeep.

Early in 1942 sponge rubber became scarce, and a substitute for cushions for these Army combat cars was required. The problem of designing a spring for this purpose was given to Universal and other spring manufacturers. Since Willys-Overland produced the Jeep, Universal had the immediate opportunity to develop a spring unit that could be substituted for the rubber cushion. This was a difficult assignment, for the rubber had been only an inch and a quarter thick. To make a

spring assembly to this specification that would have any effectiveness was not a simple design problem. Neely and Blumensaadt worked feverishly, and a solution finally occurred.
By taking small pieces of the flat, zigzag fabric, twisting it to
a vertical Z, so that it stood just over an inch high, and fasten-
ing these small sections of spring material together, a seating
unit some 18 inches square was evolved. This, in turn, was
covered with a piece of hair felt and installed in a canvas bag.
After severe tests, the seat received Army approval. It was
May 1942. The solution had taken five months.

Through this rather frantic time of creating the Jeep spring
and of adjustment, retooling, and reorganization, John Lincoln gave his unfailing support. He bore further expense and
held the conviction that the quantities of Jeeps being built and
their projected production could very well carry Universal
through the war period. The company would survive and go
on when the war ended. This gave the company's officials
courage, and Harold Neely has said, "Without that support
there is no question that the company could very quickly have
dried up and been forgotten about."

Lincoln displayed a youthful joy when he visited the plant.
He spent every available hour exploring, helping, and showing
interest in what was being done. Of these visits Neely commented, "I am reminded that in the old 69th Street plant (it
was a five-story structure) there were stairways. I can see Mr.
Lincoln now, who had reached the age of 76, running from
floor to floor. And when I say running I mean that he didn't
walk up or down the steps as one normally does. As he went
up the steps he took two at a time in order to get where he was
going in the shortest possible time. He did this repeatedly.
Everyone who witnessed this was amazed that a man of his age
could move with such agility."

Universal's wartime Jeep spring was used in all Jeeps built by Willys-Overland after 1942 and in fifty per cent of Ford-built Jeeps after 1943. Practically all tank manufacturers used the "Z" type spring during 1943, 1944, and 1945, and numerous aircraft utilized this design.

During the war, when time permitted, Universal's engineering staff applied itself to development work. When the war ended, besides continuing volume production of springs for the popular civilian Jeeps, the company was, after reconversion, in a position to apply improved methods to its other operations, to turn out superior spring seats, and to institute important economies.

Readjustment following the war brought the legal talent of William H. Bemis and the administrative and organizational ability of Chester A. Thompson into play in the company's behalf. Thompson invested in the company, and, in anticipation of greater sales in the automotive line, there was a strengthening of finances and a broadening of the organization. With Harold Neely, Bemis and Thompson put the company in order so that all outstanding debt was paid.

Most encouraging negotiations developed with General Motors. Neely and Bemis met with GM officials, seeking a way to permit both companies to produce the Universal construction. GM had in the works what was called a "light Chevrolet." While GM elected to discontinue its development after about two years, its prototypes incorporated a final seating based on the Universal spring. Naturally, this was brought to the attention of people high in General Motors and Fisher Body.

Neely, Bemis, and Thompson continued talks with GM representatives, and in October 1947 entered into a royalty license agreement whereby GM could use, sell, and manufacture Universal's product. General Motors agreed to have Universal manufacture an allocated portion of their requirement. Both obtained rights and protection regarding any new development in seating by either company, and Universal the right to offer these products to any other automotive manufacturer. Once this agreement had been reached, immediate planning started, aimed at production of front seats for a new Chevrolet and Pontiac body to be introduced as a 1949 model. This involved immediate and tremendous expansion.

John C. Lincoln was kept informed of company progress and problems, and, as always, spent considerable time amid the excitement of plant operations or listening carefully and patiently to the most detailed and difficult problems of policy and operations during his Cleveland visits. It should be emphasized that even going into the production phase for Chevrolet was not an assurance that Universal had at last achieved a stable peacetime production period or that the years which had been essentially background and development were over. Yet Lincoln was somehow assured. Recently Harold Neely recalled, "There was no question in Mr. Lincoln's mind that we would make the deadlines and go on from there. On one occasion, after we had gotten along with General Motors and were setting up facilities, he said to me, 'Well, Harold, you know I'm satisfied now that several millionaires are going to be made out of this business that we've started here.' This indicates the kind of confidence that Mr. Lincoln maintained all through the development period and into the productive period which we were fast approaching."

Universal managed to tool up and accomplish the numerous requirements to meet its deadlines in late October 1948. The first designs for GM were so thoroughly engineered that they carried through for three years.

In 1950 Universal developed the front seats for Buick and Oldsmobile. So solid was Universal's advance that its operations moved into a group of buildings in Bedford, Ohio, which gave ample space for any anticipated production. On the occasions when Lincoln visited the new plant, he was busy watching operations, studying things he thought could be improved. He would talk to the officers to obtain their ideas on what they hoped to accomplish and methods not yet resolved. Harold Neely has observed, "Without our having full knowledge that he was picking up ideas or that he was listening most carefully to the things we said, he would later surprise us. He carried away ideas when he left for Phoenix about Labor Day. He apparently had a very definite idea about setting up a project for some kind of machine or process during the winter months. The first indication that something was afoot would be our receipt of some miscellaneous billing for bearings or a motor or a gear from the Valley Machine Works in Phoenix, where he found Carl H. Schelin who could readily interpret his ideas into mechanical form. The billing would go on throughout the winter months, and usually in the springtime we would receive the shipment of a sizeable package. Uncrating the shipment, we'd find a complete machine with a motor attached, ready to be hooked up. In most cases, by inserting a wire in one end of the machine, the finished result that he was after or that we were after would emerge from the other side of the machine. This was not a thing that was done on one occasion, but at least half a dozen times during the period between Mr. Lincoln's 80th and 90th birthdays."

In 1951, returning to Pontiac and Chevrolet, Universal turned out the back-seat-spring designs. The following year it was rear seating for Buick and Olds, and in 1953 Universal springs went into the front seats of Cadillacs. With rear seating for Cadillacs in 1954, the Universal zigzag spring served all passenger cars in the General Motors line.

The furniture spring received greater attention in 1955. Although the men at Universal recognized the potential of the Universal spring types in the furniture field, general resistance by manufacturers to a simplified spring arrangement had curtailed greater efforts in this line. But with automotive application a proven success, the market began to open. With a satisfactory financial structure, greater endeavor was channeled into the complex field of upholstered furniture and a large part of Universal's development effort was directed to furniture. Sales from this pursuit exceed an annual figure of $1 million, and prospects in the field are most promising.

Company profits from the automotive lines have grown steadily, making possible a program of diversification over several years, lessening dependence on automotive spring production. This has been done by acquiring a number of subsidiaries—the Los Angeles Spring Bed Company, the Dayton Precision Manufacturing Company and the Beatrice Steel Tank Manufacturing Company—and interests in several other companies. Total sales from the parent and subsidiary companies top an annual $15 million mark.*

Before his death in the spring of 1959, John Lincoln could take satisfaction in the soundness of his judgment long ago—in 1937 when he saw a future in producing lighter, more durable, and less expensive springs. He had put his faith in an idea and had never veered from its support. Those who knew him over these years in this enterprise witnessed time and again this abiding quality. In a memorial resolution the officers of Universal paid John C. Lincoln a gracious tribute:

* In 1960 Universal was merged with Hoover Ball and Bearing Company and is currently operated as a division of that company.

This company owes John Lincoln a great debt. He organized this enterprise in 1937 [at] a time when money would buy a great deal. How remarkable that at such a time any man should interest himself in finding new ways of bending wire to make better seats. Between 1937 and 1947 he contributed over $550,000 to this Company's support and development. He collaborated with our President, Harold Neely, in the perfection of its product and in the design of machines and tools. . . . He did these things not from a desire merely of making money. There were easier ways of doing that. He did these things out of a restless urge to devote his talents and resources to making something useful and thus in a small degree to making a better world. This company would not exist today without that help from John Lincoln. . . .

Prelude to Chapter XI

FOR reasons which I shall presently elaborate, the year 1935 should be regarded as a momentous turning point in American history. It marked the end of the seventh decade since the end of the Civil War. It also saw the celebration of the sixty-ninth birthday of John C. Lincoln and the initiation of new enterprises and activities which indicated his awareness of the changes which had affected his life's interests.

The transformation of American life had been spectacular. Epoch-making inventions and the practical applications of earlier concepts changed the face of the nation and the habits and occupations of its people.

One aspect of the revolution was the shift of the economy from agriculture to industry. The developments which caused this had immeasurably raised the living standards of the people, an improvement which continued despite the blight of the great depression.

New conveniences and tools had lifted burdens from the life of the individual. New forms of employment had appeared. Changes in the means of transportation and communication had taken place. Electricity and the internal combustion engine made possible these means of drawing people closer together. Those decades had seen the coming of the telephone and radio. The motion picture had opened new avenues of contact. The automobile and later the airplane had revolutionized travel. To use a well-worn expression, the nation had become a smaller, more compact place, with a society integrated as never before. Medical science had lengthened lives and had made human suffering measurably less.

With this change, new uses had been found for government. There was an expansion of government authority—local, state, and, later, national. Cities, states, and, subsequently, the Federal government offered more services to the people, services which hitherto had been left to individual efforts of religious, philanthropic, and cooperative agencies. Ultimately, these services assumed the form of state welfarism, a manifestation which had already appeared in Britain, Germany, and other European countries.

A second component in the expansion of government was intervention in economic relationships through an authority vaguely called its police power. The free market was restricted by many and various regulations. The Wagner Act protected, even promoted, the growth of unions. These interventions were undertaken and supported by the public in the name of economic and social justice. Cities created new regulations through licensing and inspection. States set up commissions and boards of various sorts to restrict or prevent monopolistic practices.

There was also a tendency in various proposals and measures, notably in the agricultural states of the Midwest and West, to use the authority embodied in the constitutional grant to the Federal government "to coin money and regulate the value thereof."

It will simplify an explanation of the growth of government authority to identify these three avenues of intervention as: the promotion of individual welfare, the regulation of agriculture and business, and the management of the flow of money and thus the redistribution of wealth through monetary control. All three, especially the first two of these, became the objectives of the political movement generally designated as Progressivism. That exciting political ferment originated at the turn of the century and extended to the First World War. Its appeal to the essential humane instincts and the quest for economic justice was accentuated by the excesses and corruption in business life which accompanied the great expansion of the decades following the Civil War. It relied, perhaps with too much confidence, on the belief that government could provide all of the necessary authority to achieve its ends. It attracted powerful and articulate leaders and crystallized in the creating of the Progressive Party headed by Theodore Roosevelt.

To a very large degree the New Deal of Franklin D. Roosevelt was merely a revival of the Progressivism of two decades earlier.

A word of explanation should be added concerning the third method of reform stated above, the use of Federal power to stimulate the economy and redistribute wealth. This is done, or rather attempted, by the use of the authority to regulate the money supply and also by the taxing power. It is interesting to note the lineal connection between Populist demands for cheap money in the 1870s and the Keynesianism of the liberal Democrats in the 1960s.

The way to make the poor rich and to stimulate the economy—so vividly but naively explained by William Jennings Bryan in his campaigns for President—was to add to the supply of money. This was proposed to be done through issuing greenbacks without gold backing and also by raising the value of silver by free coinage.

Until the Administration of President Hayes, the greenbacks issued in the Civil War were in circulation and new issues were demanded by vociferous factions in the agricultural states. In 1876 a Greenback Labor Party began a short life. But in 1873 Congress demonetized silver. This caused a terrific uproar, and for many years that action of Congress was called "the crime of 1873." The Populist Party made the remonetization of silver a major issue, and in 1892 it mustered a million votes. Also, the Populists advocated a progressive income tax and actually secured the passage of an act by Congress providing for it in 1894. But the next year the Supreme Court held it to be unconstitutional. Various acts were passed conceding something to the silver advocates by silver purchasing by the government.

But in the McKinley Administration the discoveries of new world supplies of gold, together with a firm check on inflation and rising prosperity, ended the silver agitation.

The demand for a Federal income tax by constitutional amendment remained, however, and after the recommendations of both Presidents Roosevelt and Taft, the Sixteenth Amendment was proposed, passed, and finally ratified in 1913. The conservative supporters of the measure, however, failed to realize what a mighty instrument it would provide, not only for the redistribution of wealth but for adding to the money supply by encouraging deficit spending. The extent of this is indicated by the rise in the Federal debt from $22 billion in 1933 to $48 billion in 1940.

In the widespread demand at the outset of the Roosevelt Administration for raising prices, especially of farm products, there appeared once more senatorial advocates of "something for silver." Roosevelt measurably met the demand by limited silver purchases. But other ways were by that time available to accomplish the desired end. The budget had been unbalanced since the fiscal year 1931, and each year that passed new billions were added to the national debt. This, of course, had a decisive inflationary effect. And inflation is, in itself, a means of redistributing wealth.

This momentum was accentuated in 1935 when Roosevelt proposed and secured the enactment of drastic new increases in income tax rates.

In that same year, 1935, several circumstances moved Roosevelt to shift his attention from agriculture to the large urban centers and to the powerful minorities there. It is proper to note that with this change the First New Deal ended and the Second New Deal began.

Pure political strategy dictated much of this change. For it was apparent that the balance of political power was shifting rapidly with the population to the large urban centers. Organized labor was growing stronger, and in 1935 the CIO was formed. This vertical form of unionism was almost immediately involved in politics, and its support for the Democratic Party was a valuable addition. Minority groups, especially the Negroes newly migrated from the South and largely clustered in the cities, were becoming politically conscious. Roosevelt conceived the idea of transforming the Democratic Party from its traditional dependence upon the states'-rights South into an amalgam of minority groups chiefly centered in the urban areas. Roosevelt also became restless at the slow rate of recovery which had attended more orthodox means of stimulating economic growth.

His attention from 1935 onward was a complete reversal of his earlier concern for reviving agriculture through a national system of planning plus mere relief measures for urban distress. Policies now aimed at winning votes and support where they could be gained in large blocs.

Relief of a temporary sort became built-in welfarism in the social-security system. Labor was supported through the Wagner Act. More rights for Negroes were made a policy of Roosevelt's Administration. Larger and larger government outlays were given to government power projects in the West. Sympathetic references to countries threatened by Nazi imperialism in Europe won rich rewards among immigrant groups in the large cities in the North and Northeast.

That this change in policies was richly rewarding is shown in the results of the election in 1936, when large majorities in the big cities won him a smashing re-election.

Despite the urging of advisers to adopt the spending policies known chiefly by the name of John Maynard Keynes, Roosevelt sought to cut back the Federal deficit in his 1937 budget. But since a recession set in, probably unrelated to these economy gestures, Roosevelt after that year turned to this new brand of economic policy.

It was relatively easy to combine deficit spending with welfarism and with the building of large public improvements. Theoretically, the economy was stimulated by the distribution of more funds and the redistribution of income through high taxes and inflation. "The people" had more to spend, and thus the rate of consumption was increased.

But whether this stimulation by the government was an adequate substitute for the normal increases brought about by more public confidence in the value of the dollar is doubtful.

At any rate, the measure which is so often used to determine the rate of economic growth, the gross national product, denied the efficacy of Roosevelt's conversion to Keynesian economics. For a while, as we have noted, the GNP grew in the years 1933–1936 inclusive at the rate of 11.5 per cent a year, the rate in the succeeding four years was only 2.5 per cent a year. Unemployment fell in the first Roosevelt term from approximately 13,000,000 to 9,000,000. But in his second term it rose by 300,000.

The immense impact of the war in the 1940s ended all such experimentation and dedicated the Administration to a quite different objective than domestic reform.

But from those final years in the 1930s until now, the concepts of welfarism, high taxes, and deficit financing have become basic principles of the dominant liberal wing of the Democratic Party. Their influence was considerable in the Republican Administration of President Eisenhower, although they were never wholly adopted then.

That this represents a major turn in the nation's economic affairs goes without saying. It represents a vast area of intervention by government in the private economy.

Chapter XI

BAGDAD

IN THE summer of 1944 John C. Lincoln struck out on a fresh, bold venture by taking control of the Bagdad copper properties, located some 110 miles northwest of Phoenix. Some time before, Gordon Macklin, a Cleveland friend and a stockbroker, had interested him in a small block of Bagdad stock. After investigating particulars of the operation, Lincoln decided to buy the controlling interest in the 8,300 acres of patented land and unpatented mining claims at Bagdad and to attack the copper-mining business in earnest.

He had recognized a good opportunity and a tempting challenge and seized them. "He didn't like to see failure in a business that might be a success," Mrs. Lincoln explains.

And when John C. Lincoln took over Bagdad, it was quite certainly a failure. In 1940 E. B. Bronson, a financier and one of the original organizers of the Bagdad mine in 1907, wrote *Ebb History of Bagdad*. He tells a story of failure, generally flavored with strong traces of mismanagement. It is a strange saga, a financial quest to take an estimated thirty million tons of ore from the brown hills of Bagdad.

In 1883 John Lawler of Prescott paid two prospectors $200 for their Hawkeye and Bagdad claims, and then prospected six more claims on his own. In 1907 financier Bronson, six mining engineers, and two mining attorneys organized themselves under the laws of the Territory of Arizona as the Copper Creek Development Company. This syndicate bought Lawler's eight patented mining claims in the Eureka Mining District for $150,000.

But Lawler's luck was the beginning of the syndicate's end. There were more than thirty-three years of failure that involved at least four reorganizations and as many stock manipulations. Accompanying early attempts to "raise additional working capital" there was exploration but no production of copper. In 1911 an engineer named A. H. Rogers reported 8000 feet of tunnel work, prospecting shafts, and pits, and ninety-one churn drill holes. On the strength of the Rogers report another Arizona mining firm, Adolph Lewisohn & Sons, became involved in option agreements and further exploration, but when the World War broke out it ceased development work and finally dropped its options.

In March 1918, under another stock manipulation, the Bagdad Copper Company sold all its property and assets to Arizona-Bagdad Copper Company. Though proceeds from the sale of 350,000 mining shares were used "for corporate maintenance and development work" between 1918 and 1924, still no copper came from the mine. Then, on July 1, 1924 Arizona-Bagdad entered into an option agreement with the M. A. Hanna Co. of Cleveland which hoped to develop a leaching process for the recovery of copper. The Hanna Company spent over $200,000 on their process and a complete report on the property, which indicated that with the additional expenditure of $500,000 for mine development and metallurgical research Bagdad could be readied for open-pit mining at a further cost of $15 million. But this sort of financing was not available, and Bronson was compelled to resort to his standard solution, another stock manipulation, this time by forming the Bagdad Copper Corporation and entering into agreements with Arizona-Bagdad. By September 1929, new cash was obtained. But in October the stock market crashed.

From 1929 to 1935 Bagdad was closed down completely. Bronson pursued abortive schemes until, in 1935, he found it expedient to furnish additional working capital "along the same lines as in the past, namely the purchase and resale of donated shares which had been created for that purpose." With this financing Bagdad reported its first actual copper production, which rose to 1,537,396 pounds in 1937. But there were no profits.

At this point two investigators from the Securities Exchange Commission called at Bagdad's New York offices to inquire why the price of Bagdad stock was selling higher than a year before. SEC quickly concluded that Bagdad had created a "new issue," subject to registration. Consequently the directors filed a registration statement which brought on a hearing on the grounds of 115 deficiencies.

The Washington hearing was suddenly terminated by the dramatic resignation of two directors, Severance A. Millikin and Frank C. Page. They attacked Bronson, accusing him before the stockholders of using his position to make secret personal profits for himself. Millikin assumed control of the company in March 1938 and closed down the mine for seventeen months. At the same time, Bronson was indicted by a Federal grand jury for violation of various Federal statutes.

With low production, Bagdad reported a profit of $1,054 in 1940. And since the war effort involved greater domestic mining, the Reconstruction Finance Corporation moved in with a $2.5 million loan to equip Bagdad for the production of twenty million pounds of copper annually. In early 1942 construction of camp facilities, a new shaft, new crushing equipment, a water supply line from Burro and Boulder Creeks, and a power line from Parker Dam on the Colorado were begun. The mine lost $62,628 that year and, though the records show nothing for 1943, in the first six months of 1944 the mine lost $99,884. On August 21 John C. Lincoln acquired controlling interest in what had been described as "an investment rathole."

He moved quickly, bringing in mining engineer Ernest Dickie to take over the management of Bagdad and George Colville, a civil engineer, to assist. Then he boarded a train in Cleveland with Mrs. Lincoln and headed for Phoenix.

The route to Bagdad from the Lincoln home in Paradise Valley, over which the Lincolns traveled so many times in the fifteen years that followed, is the main highway to Wickenburg, fifty miles away. Then there is a good secondary highway for a while, then a country dirt road of twenty-one miles to Hillside. Beyond that are twenty-three miles of mountainous but paved road to Bagdad. Over this route one is climbing all the way from the elevation of 1,080 feet in Phoenix over the Grayback Mountains, and then down to Bagdad which has an elevation of 3,800 feet.

Along some of this route the Arizona Highway Patrol have placed eight white crosses as a warning to travelers that there have been deaths occasioned by cars slipping over the edge of the road. One must wind his way through the hills covered with sahuaro, cholla, and a variety of other cactus. The landscape is relieved by no trees save some small, scrubby types, mostly mesquite. The mine lies west of the town and slightly downhill.

When John C. Lincoln drove Mrs. Lincoln to the site, she recalls, "We found as poor a mining camp as you could imagine." Pitiful groups of shacks huddled around the Bagdad mine shaft. "The government had put up very cheap housing for the workers. Twenty-five men, women, and children were using one outdoor toilet."

Immediately Lincoln went to work to step up production and simultaneously to change completely the living conditions at Bagdad. In 1945, the first year of operation under Lincoln, the mine netted $31,061. But, Gordon Macklin told stockholders in the annual report of March 1946, Bagdad's underground mining was too costly and Lincoln and Dickie were developing the open-pit method of mining. "The change cost a great deal of money," Macklin explains, "and caused production to drop off materially. This naturally depleted the working capital of the company."

Lincoln had decided in late 1945 on a complete switch from underground to open-pit mining, to be financed by himself, not the RFC which had no faith in the open-pit idea. By early 1947 he had installed a pit-crusher system, "glory-hole" ore bin, and a conveyer-belt system to carry crushed ore from the pit to the mill. Whereas the company netted $321,020 in 1946, its net fell to $293,000 in 1947. Lincoln and the stockholders felt the burden of the RFC loan. Until that $2.5 million could be paid off, stockholders could receive no dividends, and retirement of the loan ate into profits.

In 1949 Lincoln reported the purchase of a fourth ball mill. "We're making an effort," he told stockholders, "to recover a larger amount of the copper in our oxide ore."

Bagdad's normal process was to carve ore from the open pit, crush it, remove waste through a flotation process, extracting a dark, sand-like concentrate. This was trucked across twenty-eight miles of mountains to a railroad spur and then hauled to an El Paso, Texas, smelter. Today, near the new town of Bagdad, the mountain has been scarred by bulldozers, and brown gashes mar the integrity of the hills. At the mine site, all around the crusher, the conveyer belts, and the mill, there rise the benches of the open-pit operation. Dynamite crews blast into the mountain. Huge electric shovels load trucks with the blasted rock.

Some of the rock is "overlay" and is hauled away to the west where it lies in great bluish masses, building each month into an increasingly large mountain of its own. To the east and south of the mill lies a large aquamarine lake, "the tailing pond," that receives the waste water and sand from the milling operation.

Lincoln knew that for each pound of copper in the concentrate shipped out, Bagdad paid a freight bill for two pounds of nothing. How much better it would be to produce pure copper at the site! He concluded that he could produce electrolytic copper from vast stockpiles of low-grade ore that had heaped up through the years as waste material, and his inventive mind came up with a method. An *Arizona Republic* reporter described Lincoln's electrolytic process in 1957:

> A tall cylindrical roasting oven converts the copper in the concentrate into a water and acid soluble form. From the roaster, the copper flows next door into a tank house for the electrical process. In a series of low tanks, thin copper "starter sheets" are used as conductors, fresh copper collecting on them the way moss clusters on stones.
>
> When a starter sheet is lowered into a tank it weighs some six pounds. Hoisted out eight days later, the ready slab runs from 85 to 100 pounds of almost pure copper. It needs no smeltering. It can be sold directly to a fabricator.

Then, with a by-product of the electrolytic process, sulfuric acid, copper can be dissolved or "leached out" of several million tons of ore stockpiled and dumped in one end of a canyon at Bagdad. Financing for the first part of this project was acquired in the spring of 1960.

In 1951 the Lincolns moved to a modest cinder-block home which commanded a view of the whole bright new town, the terraced brown mountain, the blue-green hills of copper-oxide ore, and the aquamarine tailing pond.

No longer did the shacks around the Bagdad mine shaft serve to house miners and their families. They had moved over the hill where there are neat homes scattered along the ridges, a modern shopping center, a modern school, three churches, a hospital, and first-rate recreation facilities.

On January 1, 1953 the RFC loan was paid off, and in 1954 Bagdad paid dividends for the first time in history, 25 cents a share, and a year later the company reached an all-time high in net profits: $1,886,405, declaring a dividend of 50 cents per share. Earnings were $3.48 per share. Bagdad was the fifth largest copper producer in the state, after Phelps-Dodge, Magma, Kennecott, and Inspiration.

In early 1957 Lincoln discussed his pilot plant for the production of electrolytic copper: "The plant now regularly produces about 3,000 pounds of electrolytic copper per day. This is the normal capacity of the plant.... The sulfuric acid produced by the electrolysis of two pounds of copper in the electrolytic plant will enable us to get an extra one pound of copper from our oxide ore dumps which we cannot recover at present."

In 1957 Lincoln announced that a fifth ball mill was completed that would give Bagdad a twenty-five per cent increase in income. And on March 25, 1959, just two months before his death, Lincoln's report to the stockholders was filled with hopes for the future. "The pilot plant having been operated successfully," he said, "we are endeavoring to obtain finances sufficient to enable us to enlarge the pilot plant and place such conversion on a commercial basis.

"If the company had an electrolytic plant in operation at Bagdad, it is estimated that the company would save at least five cents a pound in the cost of making electrolytic copper," said Lincoln. Figuring that Bagdad now produces twenty-three to twenty-four million pounds of copper a year, this could mean a gain of from $1,150,000 to $1,200,000 a year.

Such was the zest, energy, and vision of ninety-two-year-old John C. Lincoln.

"You should have seen him around the mine," said Mrs. Bobbie Phillips, secretary to George Colville, now manager at Bagdad. "Every morning Mr. Lincoln would open up every piece of mail—junk mail, every kind of mail—read it, and scatter it all around him on the floor.

"Then he would walk from the office down to the mill and back again before lunch. On his tours around the mountain and terraces, mills, and shops Lincoln wouldn't miss a thing."

George Colville declared, "He'd peer into the garage and observe, 'Half the trucks are in the hospital this morning. How come?' he would say. 'How come we've got so many sick trucks?' "

Chapter XII

A CONCEPT OF CHRIST
AND HIS MISSION

As we have seen, John C. Lincoln was a child of deeply religious parents—his father, William Elleby, a passionately zealous preacher in the Congregationalist faith; his mother, devout and kindly tolerant. In the household in which Lincoln spent the first nineteen years of his life their characters were engraved upon him and the spiritual matters of which they talked at length were indelibly etched into his mind. His ultimate make-up resembled that of his mother, a person of good will—benevolent, tolerant, never authoritarian.

Although with such antecedents and in such an environment religion occupied a very special place in his thinking, in neither his scientific interests nor his conception of what was right and just was he blindly conformist. In all his occupations his mind sought a rational order.

Also, his childhood and youth assured him a familiarity with the Bible. One can picture long evenings in the course of William Elleby's wandering ministry dominated by discussions between father and son. We can imagine the brilliant boy's questioning of his father on faith, doctrine, and morality.

After he left his father's house—over the many years that followed—despite his intense interest in problems in engineering and business, he spent abundant time in pondering the relations of religion with the life around him, the nature of the society in which he lived and the nature of man, his mission, and his destiny. Comprehensive familiarity with the Bible came from his lifelong reading of it.

Late in life, in his seventies, he undertook to put his religious conclusions on paper. He had long entertained such a project. Then, during three years, at odd moments while laboring at Bagdad, he wrote down ideas as they came to him. His wife remembers, "It may have been about a year that he took actual morning time to get his ideas into shape for publication."

The result is a book of 134 pages entitled *Christ's Object in Life*, privately printed and distributed by the Henry George School of New York.* In the preface Lincoln modestly disclaims pretensions to erudite scholarship or practiced writing. He says simply, "This book is an effort to show that Christ's object in life was to establish a new and better society, and that while his efforts were temporarily defeated, he has left us a revelation of the only way the Kingdom of Heaven can be brought to this earth."

Those who have delved into the enormous literature on the New Testament and the endless disputation concerning what Jesus actually taught and how His followers and Christian leaders interpret His message have usually experienced utter confusion. Cultures, nationalities, personalities, and politics have roiled the mixture.

Lincoln's book escapes this confusion. He pushed through the host of authorities straight to the heart of the gospel itself.

* The book can be obtained from the Henry George School of Social Science, 50 East 69th Street, New York City.

There is mention of only four books bearing on the New Testament, and only one of these, Canon B. H. Streeter's *The Four Gospels*, receives more than passing mention. Lincoln's argument rests predominantly upon his own interpretation of the scripture.

First, Lincoln places emphasis on the first three "synoptic gospels"—Mark, Matthew, and Luke. The first to appear, about thirty years after the death of Christ, was Mark. Matthew and Luke appeared "ten or twenty" years later. These, with only slight differences, are consistent one with the others. But the Fourth Gospel, bearing the name of John (Lincoln says "by an unknown author"), appeared some decades later. It was apparently written in the Greek city of Ephesus and is addressed to Greek readers, with Greek rather than Jewish traditions in mind.

The three synoptic gospels are in the tradition of history and biography. Luke, the Greek physician and scientist, wrote in the tradition of the great Greek historians, but with his facts carefully gleaned from witnesses of Christ's life and with the texts of Mark and Matthew before him. On the other hand, as Canon Streeter puts it, the Fourth Gospel does not belong to the literature of history but of "devotion." Lincoln calls it an "essay" with such facts drawn from the earlier gospels as were appropriate to John's argument and exploration.

Therefore Lincoln states bluntly, "In most respects the synoptics and John are complementary. In some respects they are inconsistent. Where there is inconsistency the Christian church in general has rejected the synoptics and accepted John. This writer accepts the synoptics and rejects John."

Lincoln places the writings and teaching of Paul in the same category as John. Lincoln notes that after Christ had appeared to Paul as in a vision on the road to Damascus, he retired to Arabia for three years where he formulated the system of theology which he preached with such great vigor until his death in 62 A.D. Paul and other Christians in the First Century believed and taught that Jesus would return in a relatively few years and establish the Kingdom of God on Earth. Since there would be too little time to bring about a reform, the paramount duty of the Christian was to bring himself into harmony with the spirit of God as it was embodied in Christ and await the early coming of the Redeemer. Lincoln leans toward a school of criticism which holds that the teaching of Paul was not in complete harmony with that of Jesus. Paul's teaching, according to that school, was a mystical conception of Christ which stressed the celestial personality of Christ as the Messiah and the redemption of mankind from its guilt by His sacrifice on the cross. In short, Paul's teaching and theology were largely drawn from the prophecies and beliefs of the Judean tradition while the teaching of Jesus was universal in its appeal.

Lincoln devotes two chapters, nearly a third of his book, to what is called in theology the doctrine of atonement. This is logical since the question he poses in the title is "What was Christ's real purpose in life?" One answer, held by orthodox Christianity since the days of Paul, is that aside from his moral teachings Christ was sent by God to provide a living sacrifice as atonement for the sins of mankind.

This doctrine of atonement had its origin long before the Christian era. Its roots go back even before Judaism to ancient mythology. In essence it holds that in some remote past, as exemplified in the Biblical story of Adam's disobedience and fall from grace, mankind had greatly offended God. Thus mankind incurred a massive penalty, including the temptations, vicissitudes, and mortality which afflicts human life.

146

Only a massive sacrifice by someone with divine, sinless character could expiate this load of sin. Christ, the only begotten son of God, was sent to this earth to be that sacrifice. Since He shared Godship He knew this was His terrible mission and He voluntarily assumed it.

In the early Christian era this doctrine, always essentially the same, was embellished with many details by specific churchmen. The interpretation of St. Irenaeus is an example. He said that Christ, after rejecting the temptation of Satan on the mountain, proposed a bargain. He would give Himself to Satan to have and to hold after death if Satan would in turn release his sovereignty over mankind. Satan agreed but had no intention of keeping his side of the deal. He believed that with Christ safely in his custody in Hell, he could continue his sway over mankind. To expedite the consummation he induced Judas to betray Christ and the Sanhedrin to condemn Him to death. But when Jesus died on the cross His divinity was revealed and He thereafter burst the gates of Hell and released the patriarchs and prophets imprisoned therein. But since Jesus had fulfilled His side of the bargain, mankind was thereafter free to follow Christian teaching and to participate in Christ's glory.

Lincoln holds that Jesus knew nothing of the doctrine of atonement or at any rate did not teach it. He says further that any words put in His mouth in the three synoptic gospels were interpolated therein by those who wrote the books after the crucifixion. Those writers were so impregnated by the traditions and atmosphere of the time that it seemed a matter of fair inference that Jesus believed in atonement and His mission as Messiah to die for mankind. But in so doing the writers of the synoptics enmeshed themselves in a denial of such inferences.

Lincoln's assertions that Jesus did not actually teach atonement and did not conceive His mission to die for the sins of mankind are:

1. That the conception of Christ as a suicide is inconsistent with the context of His life and conduct;

2. That since He had been so successful in three short years of teaching, He must have believed that, in the years He might have anticipated at the age of thirty-three, He would be able to accomplish much, much more;

3. That since He had been betrayed by Judas and could anticipate the punishment of death, He prayed at Gethsemane to be spared;

4. That since the apostles quarreled while on the way to Jerusalem over the offices they would hold in the new dispensation, they, too, were unaware of any inevitable tragedy;

5. That if Jesus had told the apostles of His destiny through death, He must have also told them of His resurrection. But, as Lincoln says, they "were unbelieving and dumfounded" when told of the resurrection by the women who had seen the empty sepulcher on that Sunday morning.

It is not surprising, considering the very practical character of his education and the small time he had for reading during his busy life, that Lincoln apparently knew little of the great Peter Abelard. But it is very much to his credit that his rejection of the doctrine of atonement brings him close to that most brilliant of the theologians of the eleventh and twelfth centuries.

Abelard's life is the dramatic story of a highly gifted philosopher and theologian whose independent views brought upon him the wrath of the traditionalists and ultimately of the Roman Church. But his skill in dialectic and his illuminating lectures attracted great numbers of the best students of his time. No fewer than fifty bishops, of whom twenty-five became cardinals and one was elected Pope, were students of Abelard. To a degree his work was the forerunner of a rationalization of the Christian faith which culminated in that of Thomas Aquinas. He is remembered as a man of vision in an age of challenge whose humane, rational views of religion have lived through the centuries.

Most important in the development of Abelard's thought was his conflict with Anselm, later St. Anselm, who, though his teaching was mainly carried on in France, is renowned because he attained the rank of Archbishop of Canterbury. Anselm held with some modifications the orthodox view of the doctrine of atonement, that God was offended by the sin of Adam, that God's justice demanded atonement, that such atonement could only be satisfied by the sacrifice of one who was both God and man, and that Christ's voluntary martyrdom satisfied that requirement.

This theory was challenged by Abelard while a student under Anselm at Laon. Abelard found no rational explanation, he said, for God, the all-powerful, to permit Satan to become the master of mankind. Man had sinned only against God, and it was within the power of God to forgive him. To Abelard it made no sense to say that the sins of mankind could be expiated by the crowning sin of murdering Christ who was doing God's work. If God is good, how could He find satisfaction in the sacrifice of an innocent man? Thus Abelard rejected the traditional theory of atonement and stated instead his concept of Christ's mission in life. This was, he said, to make men know better the nature of God's mercy and to inspire them in a love of God. He demonstrated His love for men by His teaching, His pure life, and the terrible risk He assumed in braving even death with fortitude for the sake of this mission. Redemption is achieved within man himself by contemplating the example of Christ, not by bloody sacrifice.

It is Lincoln's distinction that by his own reading of the gospels, by his capacity to use reason as a means to the end, and by the essential humanity of the man, he reached practically the same conclusions as Abelard.

Lincoln held further that Jesus at the height of His influence as a teacher of God's word noted that His disciples recognized Him as the promised Messiah of the Jewish people. Therefore, Jesus thought that the masses of the Jewish people would also recognize Him as such and accept His leadership in their religion. He was not interested in a temporal revolution against the rule of Rome but in a spiritual renaissance signalized by the overthrow of the Sanhedrin. Accordingly, He planned and executed a triumphal entry into Jerusalem.

His plans were frustrated by Judas's betrayal. Lincoln explains Judas's action by stating that he did not anticipate the condemnation and death of Jesus. He was interested in something far more substantial than the thirty pieces of silver. He was ambitious and hoped to become keeper of the treasury under a regime in which Jesus would be the head. Since he knew that Jesus was capable of performing miracles, he believed that with defeat and death facing Him, Jesus would use His powers to defeat His enemies and rescue Himself. As proof, Lincoln cites the behavior of Judas after the deed was done. When Jesus did not perform the expected miracle, Judas returned the money and hanged himself.

Lincoln interprets the commandment "Love thy neighbor as thyself" as what modern writers call a "social gospel." In this he follows such modern writers and theologians as Shailer Matthews and Edgar J. Goodspeed. Henry Churchill King, long president of Oberlin College, recognized the importance of Christ's teaching to society but stressed more firmly than Matthews, Goodspeed, and Lincoln the essentially personal, individual relationship of a man to Christ and God.

The object of Christ in life is summarized by Lincoln in these words:

"In a sentence, we can say that Christ's object in life was to set up an earthly organization of which He would be the head and His apostles officers, based upon the twin foundations of the fatherhood of God and the brotherhood of man, and called by Matthew the kingdom of Heaven, and by Mark the kingdom of God."

Chapter XIII

JUSTICE THROUGH
LAND TAXATION

JESUS had the genius to see how the dreams of the ancient
prophets—dreams that the earth could be a place where
peace and righteousness and prosperity should reign—could be
realized, and He devoted His life to the task of helping other
men to see the same vision He saw and to join with Him in
bringing it to pass. The vision could not be realized without
some human organizations in which good reigned rather than
evil. . . . Can we do better than to catch part of the vision He
had and use our lives to help rid the world of evils and the
wars and poverty and broken lives that result from evil."

This is written in John C. Lincoln's book, *Christ's Object
in Life*. It is a summary statement of his faith. It was also his
abiding purpose to give in the spirit of that faith his zeal, energy, intelligence, and most of the material means which he
had accumulated over a long and productive life.

There was nothing of the mystic in Lincoln. He was a very
practical individual. He regularly attended and generously
supported the churches of his choice. But he was far more interested in the application of the Christian faith to the actuali-

ties of life, to social and political organization and public understanding that justice be embodied in law.

He was quite aware of the hard facts of life. He had lived with them many years. He understood men in their strength and weakness. But he believed that their lives could be enriched if they shared with him his belief in Christ's teaching. This he believed could be achieved by what he so often called the natural law as a rule to guide all human associations.

He wanted to apply the natural law to economic affairs. This he believed to be the way to equalize opportunities, eliminate involuntary poverty, and clear the way to social and political harmony and peace.

He could not believe in those principles of socialism which have allured so many seekers of justice. For he believed that the state had been a partner in imposing those inequitable laws which he regarded as violations of the natural law. Also he was a passionate individualist whose success had been possible because of the climate of freedom which prevailed in the United States in his time. Equality in goods imposed by a super-state seemed to him wholly inconsistent with existing inequitable laws which penalized the deserving and enriched the unworthy.

He knew the market place well and realized through experience that monopoly was a major evil, especially a monopolistic ownership of land.

These conclusions, his belief in the social implications in Christ's teachings, their application in the natural law, with freedom for individual enterprise and a realization that all forms of monopoly were inimical to equality of opportunity, he had found embodied in the teachings of the philosopher who next to Christ influenced him more than any other. That influence became an abiding reality seventy years before his death when he was working for Brush. It was in Cleveland at a meeting at which the speaker was Henry George.

George was then at the summit of his fame. His masterpiece, *Progress and Poverty*, had appeared ten years earlier, and its influence had penetrated many nations. Some estimate of George and his influence was conveyed by a notable American philosopher at the time of his death in 1897:

> No man, no graduate of a higher educational institution has a right to consider himself educated unless he has some first-hand acquaintance with the theoretical contribution of this great thinker. We find in *Progress and Poverty* the analysis of the scientific with the sympathies and aspirations of a great lover of mankind.

Henry George, who became such an abiding influence in Lincoln's life and thought, was born in Philadelphia. He was not reared in poverty, but the circumstances of his respectable family could be described as austere. At the age of fifteen, in a period of severe hard times in the 1850s, he went to sea. The impressions gained in his travels deeply affected him, for he saw grim human conditions in Calcutta and dire unemployment in Australia. Meanwhile he learned the printer's trade and developed a talent for observation and reporting. Finally his travels brought him to San Francisco where he worked at odd jobs as a printer. Frequently in those years his personal situation was so acute that he virtually lived as a tramp. But despair, worries, and want were always mingled with high purpose, idealism, and plans for the future. Before long he drifted into editorial work and, with a bit of publishing on the side, he became a writer. It was a period in California's history when there was plenty of evidence of the inequities created by land ownership. Wealth was growing through land speculation, not only in the city itself but in the profits made from the land along the new railways. But there was also profound poverty on every side. George, who was moved by deep moral imperatives, became an ardent evangelist.

His talents opened the way to editorial positions which considerably improved his personal fortunes. Financially he did rather well and he became an individual of considerable influence in the city.

After the Civil War land speculation broke out in full force. Great fortunes were growing. George gradually drew a number of conclusions. He realized that land speculation was providing vast increments for a few with little or no effort. Wealth and want were living side by side, and he concluded that the greater the accumulations of wealth the greater the depth of poverty. Then he wrote a small brochure *Our Land and Land Policy*, in which there appeared the basic conclusions later elaborated in *Progress and Poverty*. He found it possible to supplement what he learned from observation with extensive reading in the field of economics. He began a correspondence with certain classical economists, including John Stuart Mill.

In 1875 he lost his final editorial position in San Francisco and went East where he immediately began the research and writing which appeared in 1879 as *Progress and Poverty*.

The tremendous impact of this book on the generation that followed its publication was not due to the originality of the concepts which it presented. For the idea of heavier taxes on land was advocated a hundred years before by the French physiocrats. In one form or another it ran through the writings of many of the classical economists before George. His four Canons of Taxation were almost identical with those written by Adam Smith in his *Wealth of Nations* in 1776. But the eloquence of his style, the background from which he wrote, which was land exploitation in the California he knew so well, and, above all, the moral conviction of the man that he was truly expressing immutable and natural laws of justice made his contribution unique.

He rejected the collectivists' ideas of his time and stood firmly for individual enterprise unfettered by inequitable levies and monopoly. His Canons of Taxation were a plea for the encouragement of individual efforts free from the penalties imposed by traditional taxation. They were:

> The best tax by which public revenue can be raised is evidently that which will closest conform to the following conditions:
>
> 1. That it bear as lightly as possible on production . . .
> 2. That it be easily and cheaply collected and fall as directly as possible on the ultimate payers . . .
> 3. That it be certain—so as to give the least opportunity for tyranny and corruption on the part of officials and the least temptation to law breaking and evasion on the part of the taxpayers.
> 4. That it bear equally, so as to give no one an advantage or put anyone at a disadvantage as compared with others.

These principles, it will readily be seen, have even more pertinence today than when they were written. For on every side we see the immense burden of taxation on production, the mammoth bureaucracy which is employed in collection, the alarming trend toward avoidance by the rich and evasion by the poor, the host of indirect taxes imposed by political expediency by Congress, the state legislatures, and the local authorities. There is evidence on every side that under our modern network of taxation speculators are enriched while producers are sorely penalized.

George in his *Progress and Poverty* came to his conclusion that the central problem was land monopoly with singular coherence:

It is sufficiently evident that with regard to production, the tax upon the value of land is the best tax that can be imposed. Tax manufactures, and the effect is to check manufacturing; tax improvements, and the effect is to lessen improvement; tax commerce, and the effect is to prevent exchange; tax capital, and the effect is to drive it away. But the whole value of land may be taken in taxation, and the only effect will be to stimulate industry, to open new opportunities to capital, and to increase the production of wealth. . . .

The present method of taxation operates upon exchange like artificial deserts and mountains; it costs more to get goods through a custom house than it does to carry them around the world. It operates upon energy, and industry, and skill, and thrift, like a fine upon those qualities. If I have worked harder and built myself a good house while you have been contented to live in a hovel, the taxgatherer now comes annually to make me pay a penalty for my energy and industry, by taxing me more than you. If I have saved while you wasted, I am mulct, while you are exempt. If a man build a ship we make him pay for his temerity, as though he had done an injury to the state; if a railroad be opened, down comes the tax collector upon it, as though it were a public nuisance; if a manufactory be erected we levy upon it an annual sum which would go far toward making a handsome profit. . . . We punish with a tax the man who covers barren fields with ripening grain, we fine him who puts up machinery, and him who drains a swamp. How heavily these taxes burden production only those realize who have attempted to follow our system of taxation through its ramification. . . .

On the land problem he saw in his day, George was capable of highly literary exposition:

Take now . . . some hard-headed businessman, who has no theories, but knows how to make money. Say to him: "There is a little village; in ten years it will be a great city —in ten years the railroad will have taken the place of the stage-coach, the electric light of the candle; it will abound with all the machinery and improvements that so enormously multiply the effective power of labor. Will, in ten years, interest be any higher?"

He will tell you, "No!"

"Will the wages of common labor be any higher; will it be easier for a man who has nothing but his labor to make an independent living?"

He will tell you, "No!"

"What then will be higher?"

"Rent; the value of land. Go, get yourself a piece of ground and hold possession."

And if, under such circumstances, you take his advice, you need do nothing more. You may sit down and smoke your pipe; you may lie around like the lazzaroni of Naples or the Leperos of Mexico; you may go up in a balloon, or down in a hole in the ground; and without doing one stroke of work, without adding one iota to the wealth of the community, in ten years you will be rich! In the new city you may have a luxurious mansion; but among its public buildings will be an almshouse.

George proposed the following reform:

I do not propose either to purchase or to confiscate private property in land. The first would be unjust; the second, needless. Let the individuals who now hold it still retain, if they want to, possession of *their* land. Let them buy and sell, and bequeath and divide it. We may safely leave them the shell, if we take the kernel ... *It is not necessary to confiscate land; it is only necessary to confiscate rent.*

Progress and Poverty achieved immediate success. Its practical effects were tangible and of a far-reaching nature. Thoughts that Henry George had written stimulated, over an extended period of time, considerable reform of property taxes both here and abroad. The Irish fell upon his ideas, for English agrarian policy spread inflammatory resentment and revolt among their people and their political leaders. In 1881 *The New York Irish World* sent George to Ireland where his speeches were enthusiastically received.

His impact was no less significant on British thinking, for he aroused it to a greater sense of social conscience concerning the economic shortcoming of the British system. Four times during the 1880s he toured the British Isles. There he was hailed as a great social and economic reformer. *Progress and Poverty* and its author's agitation were instrumental in bringing about Lloyd George's land tax in 1909.

The encompassing land reform which George sought found its fullest application in New Zealand and Denmark, and, to a lesser degree, in Australia and Germany.

Henry George's ideas enjoyed popularity but less success in the United States. Yet he tirelessly advanced his creed through articles and speeches. In 1886 he finished another volume, *Protection or Free Trade*, which was to be widely read and inserted into the Congressional Record in six parts by one of his disciples—Tom Johnson—and five other Representatives.

That same year he ran unsuccessfully against the Tammany candidate for Mayor of New York. But behind him in the final count was the Republican candidate, Theodore Roosevelt. For ten years following this disappointment George continued his economic evangelism, touring the United States, crossing oceans to shores as distant as Australia, and writing incessantly.

In my judgment George brought home, with perhaps the most easily understood illustration, the concept of social value which inspired the whole Progressive movement in the United States in the generation which began near the dawn of the twentieth century. For anyone can see that the individual who holds a piece of land with no effort to improve it and who has small taxes to pay cannot help but be enriched by those whose industry enriches the entire community. He toils not and neither does he spin, but his land increases in value.

But the subjects George considered in his many speeches and his writings touched almost all of the corrective influences which were the result of the Progressive movement. The restriction of monopoly, more democratic political machinery, municipal reform, the elimination of privilege in railroads, the regulation of public utilities, and the improvement of labor laws and working conditions—all were in one way or another accelerated by George.

It may well be argued that the phrase "single tax," which became identified with his name, has had much to do with the neglect of George in a more recent generation. For with the growing responsibilities of government the concept of collecting all public revenues from land is subject to question and has, in fact, been derided by many responsible economists. For modern civilization offers many other instances in which social acceptance, and thus social value, provides an unearned increment to those in legally strategic positions. They too should bear a heavier share of taxation in line with George's Four Canons.

Most of those who adhere to the broad concepts of George's philosophy prefer the expression "land value taxation." This would move toward capturing much more of the rental income of land by assessments which bear equally on improved and unimproved land and which would remove some of the burden of taxes from improvements.

Henry George, the speaker at the meeting in 1889 which initiated John C. Lincoln's lifetime interest, had been brought to Cleveland by Tom L. Johnson, who was at that time a builder and owner of street railway systems as well as a steel manufacturer and capitalist. Johnson had been converted to the ideas of George some time before, and later he became the economist's foremost disciple.

As Lincoln later recalled, the meeting was attended by about five hundred people. But he also recalled that at that time he "had no idea what George was talking about." In the years immediately after, while Lincoln was working for Short, he had several contacts with Johnson, mainly because Short was interested in selling streetcars to the Johnson interests. There was no sale of streetcars, but later, when Johnson became Mayor of Cleveland from 1901 to 1910, Lincoln learned much more of George's ideas through Johnson's remarkable influence on the life of the city and his practical application of George's ideas.

Lincoln secured a copy of George's famous book, *Progress and Poverty*, and systematically read it at least three times. His earlier reading and thinking about social reform had made him acquainted with the principles of socialism, but his own common sense and experience, together with George's cogent argument against that sort of reform, convinced him that George had the better answer. Later he read other books by George.

When Lincoln was in Europe in 1913 he discussed not only engineering but economic problems. He visited many of the leading land reformers of that time. In England he was especially impressed with John Paul, who was a leader in the Single Tax movement.

In the years following that visit to Europe Lincoln came to know many of the Georgist leaders in the United States. He never met but knew about Robert Schalkenbach, a master printer in New York who established a foundation which bears his name and which is dedicated to the dissemination of George's ideas. Lincoln knew Francis Neilson, an Englishman who was head of the British League for the Taxation of Land Values and who visited the United States. Joseph Fels, a Philadelphia soap manufacturer, was also a Georgist at that time, and up to his death in 1914, was active in the movement. He left a considerable fortune to the cause.

A Commonwealth Land Party in 1924 nominated John C. Lincoln as its candidate for Vice-President on a ticket headed by William J. Wallace of New Jersey. The only purpose of that party was the promulgation of the Georgist philosophy, and Lincoln later doubted its effectiveness. Years later he said, "It was a crazy thing to do." He noted that his campaign cost him $2,000.

In the first two decades of the twentieth century, Single Tax movements grew in many countries. In the United States there were hundreds of devoted adherents. Clubs and schools were organized in several cities. But, for many reasons, the Georgist movement declined. When the great depression came in 1929, George was almost a forgotten man.

However, in 1932 Oscar H. Geiger established the Henry George School of Social Science in New York, hoping thereby to promote through educational methods more public interest in George and his ideas. The school, in the years that followed, acquired from several believers in George substantial sums for operation and endowment. Lincoln became interested in the school in 1936 and became a large contributor to its support.

After the publication of his book on Christ, Lincoln wrote a number of small treaties on land value taxation, which were distributed through the Henry George School. They were entitled, "Should Land Have Selling Value?", "Scientific Taxation," and "The Natural Source of Revenue for the Government." A final and longer one, "Stop Legal Stealing," was published a year before his death. In various forms and with apt illustrations these essays are outspoken statements of the iniquity of land monopoly, land speculation with great unearned profits, and, in a somewhat modified form, the concept of Henry George that the income from land be taken by the community which created it.

As we shall see in the next chapter, the basic argument of Henry George, as well as the contentions of Lincoln over the years, is more than justified by circumstances prevalent now. The Federal, state, and local governments contribute vast sums for urban renewal and redevelopment for housing, highway construction, and even farm subsidies, collected from the taxpayers through the income tax and other forms of levies which greatly enrich those who own land in fortunate situations. These values, created by society, become private profits, mostly unearned. As this inequity is more generally realized and remedied, the principles so earnestly expressed and supported by John C. Lincoln may indeed attain reality in the social and legal order. Lincoln often said that it might be years before the truth would prevail. This was to remain his faith, unshaken to the end.

Chapter XIV

SOCIETY GAVE
AND IS GIVEN UNTO

THE sincerity of a man's convictions is not proved by his words, however forceful or eloquent they may be. It is proved by what he is willing to give of himself and his material means. With Lincoln Christianity was no mere Sunday exercise. He lived it in everything he did.

Henry George had taught him that a man's material gains are not valuable merely because of his expenditure of toil, foresight, and intelligence, but because society has given them worth. As we have seen in the chapters of this book, Lincoln was not interested in wealth merely because of a desire for accumulation, for ostentation, or for power over others. It was something to be used for helping others and for the creation of better social and economic conditions for all.

After he had passed middle life, because of investments or because of his continuing efforts his wealth became considerable, and he devoted himself seriously to its disposition for worthy ends.

After he had decided to make Phoenix his permanent home, he first became interested in the Desert Mission at Sunnyslope,

Arizona, which had been started in the 1920s by the Presbyterian Church. Its purpose was to give assistance to indigent seekers of health.

In the past thirty years tuberculosis has been drastically reduced because of new methods of treatment as well as early detection. But in the generation before, the "white plague" was a major enemy of mankind.

In those earlier years physicians had only a rudimentary knowledge of tubercular therapy, and often after a patient's condition had progressed from bad to worse he was advised that a dry climate and a dry climate alone was his salvation. Thousands were advised to go out to the Southwest and "rough it." This usually ended in death. But constant throngs of sufferers came to the Southwest and Colorado with little to guide their treatment and nothing much to pay their way. The presence of these penniless "lungers," as they were called out there, became a major problem for public authority and private philanthropy.

In the 1920s a number of these health seekers inhabited some shacks in the desert about nine miles from Phoenix. Death was the common end of these unfortunates.

A compassionate woman, Miss Elizabeth Beatty, a retired stenographer, took an interest in the unfortunate children in the colony and began taking them to a private home for Sunday school lessons. The Presbyterian church to which she belonged took an interest, and in a few years there developed for the patients and their families a chapel, a community building, a library, and an outpatient building at Sunnyslope.

In 1933 the Lincolns found this colony and purchased twenty acres of land adjoining it. This proved to be an investment that brought dividends in help for the needy.

A convalescent cottage was erected on the Lincoln land in

1941. Then in 1942 a fire destroyed most of the buildings of the Mission and the Lincolns began in earnest to rebuild the entire establishment in a more permanent form. They made possible an administration building, an outpatient clinic, a baseball park, a swimming pool, and a day nursery which was named after Mrs. Lincoln. Lincoln then brought to the Mission an experienced executive, H. F. Hancox. The expansion of the Mission continued until Lincoln's death in 1959. The John C. Lincoln Hospital and other facilities of the Mission grew into a first-class institution, licensed by the State of Arizona and admitted to membership in the American Hospital Association. Some financial aid came from other donors, but the Mission's present form is, in major part, due to Lincoln's considerable financial contributions. Mr. Hancox tells of the occasion when it was proposed that the hospital apply for Federal assistance under legislation provided for that purpose. It was only with great reluctance on Lincoln's part that the aid was accepted. Lincoln wanted, above all, to avoid any Federal control over the project. Mr. Hancox says that Lincoln took a keen delight in giving money to the hospital himself rather than letting the Federal government do it.

During his final twenty-three years in Arizona Lincoln took an active interest in the Phoenix YMCA. He was a member of the board and he and Mrs. Lincoln were the largest contributors to the new YMCA building in downtown Phoenix. In 1938 the Lincolns built the main lodge at the YMCA camp at Prescott. Lincoln was also a member of the board of the Good Samaritan Hospital in Phoenix. He supported the activities of the Presbyterian Church which he and Mrs. Lincoln attended.

But despite these gifts to worthy philanthropic causes, Lincoln never believed that charity, in the sense in which that term is generally understood, is the major virtue in a good life. His definition of charity embodied the concept of justice, of equality of opportunity for self-help, and of a more humane social order. That was his abiding concern, and it centered in the concepts of the natural law as interpreted by Henry George.

In 1936 he became interested in the Henry George School in New York and began to make financial contributions. Largely because of Lincoln's generosity, the school purchased an old telephone building on 23rd Street. Lincoln became a member of the board of directors and later president. With the support of Lincoln and other contributors, the school acquired a substantial endowment and moved into a large building on 69th Street. It assisted in the establishment and support annually of several branches in other cities. It publishes a monthly magazine, *The Henry George News*, and offers many public lectures. Its educational work includes classes in a number of subjects. Tuition is free.

After Lincoln became interested in the school he regularly contributed to its support, in cash and by gifts of stock. After the establishment of the Lincoln Foundation, the foundation made annual grants for the school's support. Altogether, more than a million dollars of Lincoln money have been given to the school.

In 1947, at the ripe age of eighty-one, Lincoln felt that he must make plans for the projection of his faith in Henry George's ideas far beyond his own lifetime. As he often said, "It may take a hundred years before present systems of taxation will fail because they are unsound." Then, he believed, the truth must prevail. He approved of the various schools and other agencies which he supported, but they too might not endure.

And so, in 1947, he asked his attorney in Phoenix, Frank L.

Snell, to take the necessary steps to create a foundation in his name and dedicated to the ideas of Henry George. Snell, with the advice and direction of Lincoln, drew up the necessary papers, and the State of Arizona granted a charter for the Lincoln Foundation.

The purpose of the foundation, as stated in the Articles of Incorporation, is "to teach, expound and propagate the ideas of Henry George as set forth in his book, *Progress and Poverty*, in such a manner as the Board of Directors may direct."

The board is to consist of "not more than eleven and not less than nine members." Four of these were to be life members and were members of the Lincoln family—until his death, John C. Lincoln; Lillian; Joseph; and David.* The other members are elected for terms of three years by the board itself. No member shall serve more than two terms.

In the report of the foundation, published in 1958, there is incorporated a "Statement of the Founder," John C. Lincoln:

In 1947 after more than sixty active years in the fields of industry and investment I established this foundation.

Over those years I have become convinced, because of my experience in the business world and also because of what I read of economics and public affairs, of a number of vital facts. In the first place, the community by its presence and activities creates a value called ground rent. Therefore, this ground rent belongs to the community, rather than to the land-owner who, under the law as it is

---

* In 1961 the members are David C. Lincoln, Joseph C. Lincoln, Lillian Lincoln Howell, John W. Bricker, P. I. Prentice, William Feather, Graham Aldis, G. Rowland Collins, and Herbert J. Miller. The Treasurer is William H. Bemis; Secretary, Frank L. Snell; President, David C. Lincoln; Vice-President, Joseph C. Lincoln.

now written, has title to the land. When the land-owner collects ground rent, instead of the community, the community is denied its natural source of revenue and is compelled to levy taxes on the earned wealth of its citizens. This, I contend, is inequitable, and a violation of the moral law. There is an essential need that this denial of justice be made known to a wider and wider audience.

I found that the clearest and most comprehensive portrayal of these facts was in the writings of Henry George. In more recent years I have witnessed to my profound regret that the contributions of Henry George were to a greater and greater extent overshadowed by the purely empirical and materialistic philosophies of later economists, notably in our educational institutions at all levels.

I felt, therefore, that the remedy should be education, not only of the public directly but of those leaders in education and in other areas in which public opinion is shaped.

The foundation which I established was, therefore, dedicated to education in its broadest sense.

It was and is my belief that this educational effort should extend over many years and seek through the dissemination of proven truth to change the standards of economic education and of public opinion, and thus contribute to a more just and productive life for free men and women.

Since under the terms of the Articles of Incorporation the directors shall determine the manner in which the purposes of the foundation shall be carried out, the board has adopted the following statement of policy:

The Board of Directors is empowered to determine the manner in which the stated purpose of the Foundation shall be carried out. In line with this directive, the Board has recognized that Henry George in his *Progress and Poverty* presented not only an analysis and remedy related to certain ills in our civilization, but a broad treatise on the principles of economics. Those principles, notably in taxation, are in the ideological tradition of earlier economists who in their day were appropriately called "liberal." That is, they were exponents of economic liberty within nations and freedom of commerce and trade within the world. In the semantic fashion of the present day, the word "liberal" has been appropriated by those who believe in more, rather than less, governmental intervention in economic life. Thus the long line of economists from Adam Smith to Henry George would be called conservative today.

The kinship of George with Adam Smith, who published his *Wealth of Nations* almost precisely a century before *Progress and Poverty*, is shown by the identity between the four Canons of Taxation stated by both.*

It should also be noted that George's *Progress and Poverty* appeared only a few years after Karl Marx published his materialistic *Das Kapital* and that George specifically took issue with Marxian socialism. His philosophy is in direct contradiction to Marxian materialism.

George believed that the gravest expression of inequity in the laws and governmental policies of his time was in the status of land and of land taxation. Accordingly, he laid great stress upon those aspects of economics.

Hence, in fulfilling the spirit and letter of the stated purpose of the Lincoln Foundation, the Board of Directors has determined that its concern in distribution of the income of the Foundation should be in the related

* These appear on p. 156 of Chapter XIII.

fields of land ownership and taxation, as well as in removing restraints upon individual initiative and enterprise and production which exist in many other forms of taxation.

Administration policies, in the nature of things, must grow and change with experience. But the Board of Directors decided shortly after its organization that the Foundation should be a granting, rather than an operating institution. Thus the Foundation should select grantees with care and, within certain stated limits, permit them discretion in the actual operation of teaching, research and promulgation of the results thereof. It has not and does not at this time plan to operate directly in teaching, research or in the promulgation of information. Hence it has been able to conduct its affairs with a minimum of administrative overhead and thus to use its resources to the fullest possible extent upon its grants.

It has supported projects in the related fields of teaching and research. In teaching, it has supported not only adult education, but higher education in colleges and graduate schools. It has stressed the desirability that appropriate research in its specified fields shall be closely related to classroom instruction. It intends also to support and encourage public enlightenment through the publication of the results of the research it has supported, as well as the application of such results in economic instruction in schools at all levels.

The grants made by the foundation have been directed to two aspects of the general problem of education: adult education in economics, and research and teaching in colleges and universities.

In adult education the largest contributions have been to

the Henry George School in New York. These have been in line with John C. Lincoln's desire to further the development of the school's activities. The board of directors also believes that useful purposes can be furthered by direct promulgation of the ideas and written works of George.

Sizeable grants were made to the Henry George School in Chicago between the years 1953 and 1958 to support an experiment in offering courses in elementary economics in industrial plants.

A three years' grant was made to the Industrial Relations Center of the University of Chicago to develop the subject of taxation in a course designed for use in industrial plants in various cities under the direction of various colleges and universities.

A grant was made for three years to the Society for the Advancement of Management for economic courses for its members.

Grants for the support of teaching and research in higher education were made to the University of Southern California, to Claremont (California) Men's College, and to the graduate schools of business administration of New York University and the University of Virginia.

No restrictions have been made in these grants to colleges and universities, limiting their use to the promulgation exclusively of the ideas of Henry George. However, in each case it has been understood that George be adequately considered in courses dealing with the classical economists and that in research there be considered the subject of land taxation.

During this period in which the Lincoln Foundation was making the foregoing experimental grants, the officers and members of the board were considering and planning for a major enterprise which would, to a degree, consolidate its activities in one center. This concept has been the establishment of a school of public finance, with instruction at a graduate level and considerable attention to research. It has been clear that, while there is already a large amount of instruction in law schools and other institutions of higher education, there is need for concentration on the basic problems, social and economic, in taxation and other aspects of public finance. Students and graduates of such an institution might be prepared to take positions in governmental agencies, universities, tax associations, and government research organizations.

This concentration of a considerable part of the income of the foundation would tend to avoid that scatteration of activities and resources so common among foundations. Also, such a school would, through its graduates and publications, materially advance knowledge in sound economic principles, measurably improve instruction in schools and colleges, and contribute to an enlightened public opinion in a subject which vitally concerns taxpayers everywhere.

After long consideration, it was decided by the foundation board that a favorable place for the establishment of such a school would be in affiliation with Claremont Men's College, where for six years the foundation supported grants for instruction and research. The location in the associated group of colleges of Claremont and the Claremont Graduate School assures a favorable intellectual climate for study and research and also, because of its nearness to the immense metropolitan areas of Los Angeles County, an opportunity for close contacts with practical situations in economic life.

Accordingly, a contractual arrangement was concluded

and approved by the foundation board and the trustees of Claremont Men's College for the establishment of such a school, which will have its opening in 1962. It is contemplated that there will be four John C. Lincoln professors in the appropriate subjects, with ample facilities for research. Adequate emphasis will be on land taxation under the terms of the foundation charter.

This Lincoln School of Public Finance will receive a major part of the income of the foundation, which in 1961 had reached the annual total of approximately $300,000.

In any evaluation of the importance of the ideas of Henry George, it should be noted that long before he attained standing as an economist—indeed, before he had enjoyed any systematic education in economic thought (he left school at fourteen and went to sea at fifteen)—he arrived at certain basic conclusions by personal observation as a journalist in San Francisco. From those observations he arrived at certain lasting conclusions concerning the inequities embedded in the conditions and laws of his time. He saw that, despite the vast size of the state of California, the area available for human enjoyment and support was severely limited. This was especially true of the peninsula on which the city of San Francisco was located. He saw also that, because of the limitation of available water supply and means of transportation, land for cultivation was relatively small. In short, that conditions were ideally suited for the growth of monopoly in land and for the enrichment of those fortunate enough to be owners.

It was also a time when government subsidies in the form of land were available to the builders of the early railroads. From these monopolistic opportunities and from the government's lavish gifts of land to those who built the railroads vast fortunes accumulated. At the same time poverty prevailed among a great majority of the people, both in the cities and in the countryside.

It is not now true, as George contended, that poverty prevails amidst abundance in the United States. But many of the inequities which George assailed have reappeared in land ownership. Urban areas are still retained as slums by owners whose assessments are low and who are making enormous unearned profits by the outpouring of government money for housing, slum clearance, and urban renewal. Our vast new highway systems, like the railroads of George's time, are enriching land owners who happen to have holdings along their routes. For reasons best known to themselves, assessment authorities generally increase land valuations only at the expense of those who build productive improvements of their land. Over all are the vast sums spent by the Federal and state governments in acquiring unproductive land for public improvements, allegedly to help the poor by providing better housing and to beautify the cities and their environs. But such grants also provide windfalls in unearned increments.

It is also true that in farming areas where government subsidies are paid there is a tremendous inflation in land values not justified by the productiveness of the land itself. In this case inflation is a deadly peril. For if the subsidies should cease there would be a collapse which would imperil the entire national economy.

This opportunity for the gaining of unearned fortunes by land owners and speculators, as anyone can see by an inspection of the cities and suburbs, results in haphazard and uneconomical city and suburban growth. Housing develops in spots, while great areas are kept in slums in the urban areas and in weeds in suburban areas by those who expect to gain unjustifiably high prices.

Thus if ever a prophet is justified by the passage of time, it is Henry George. And that vindication deserves to be shared by John C. Lincoln, one of the most perceptive and valiant of George's disciples.

Prelude to Chapter XV

As THE first years of the 1950s unfolded we may assume that John C. Lincoln must have reviewed in perspective the amazing century over most of which his life had extended. For the one hundred years which began with the end of the Civil War will be judged in history the most remarkable and, in some ways, the greatest since the dawn of recorded time. Certainly that century will be the most outstanding in the story of America.

And its final quarter, beginning in 1940, will have seen the most fundamental changes in American life.

The onset of war for the United States in 1941 found us, as war had so often found us before, relatively unprepared. War is the business of governments, in our case of the Federal government. In the Roosevelt years politics had portrayed individual enterprise as a sort of anachronism which had entered a slow dissolution and which would be replaced by an order in which "social" concepts, values, and direction would prevail. In some areas government itself had entered into direct competition with individual enterprise on the ground that it could do the job better and more efficiently. The elite in government held that, since private enterprise could not plan for itself, government must, as a minimum contribution, plan the economy and assign the tasks to be performed therein.

The impact of war brought about a shocking awakening in the government's thinking. The immense demands of a great conflict, in which our allies were already falling back partly exhausted before superlatively organized German power, compelled the Federal Administration to turn to those whose life had been given to the production of goods of all kinds. American industry and agriculture responded. Almost at once the United States became the center of production for half the embattled world. The government, getting the money by borrowing from the savings of the American people, became a mere purchasing agent. A capitalistic industry and agriculture delivered the goods.

Aircraft were needed in almost unbelievable numbers. A small industry grew to major proportions almost overnight. In a year we had surpassed the aircraft production of Germany, Italy, and Japan and were ready for a war in which attrition was to be decisive. Ships were needed to carry arms and supplies to every world front. By 1943, 150 ships came down the ways each month. These were in large part welded by techniques which had occupied the mind of the farseeing John C. Lincoln for many years of his life. The war effort required prodigal outpouring of our mineral resources. Copper was in heavy demand, for, as a military leader said, "an army without copper would be an army without speed, maneuverability, communications, or fire power."

Our factories produced arms of all kinds, motor vehicles, and heavy machinery to make roads and airfields for allied armies. The output of petroleum, gas, and electricity grew.

On our highways great numbers of trucks appeared, and at the same time our railroads, so distressed since the onset of the depression, came to life. Food in immense quantities flowed from our harvests to hungry fighting nations in Europe and Asia.

The climactic conclusion of the struggle was marked by the appearance of the most revolutionary force of all time, atomic power. This had been produced at the government's behest through contracts with American corporations and universities. They had supplied the engineering and inventive genius which made the atom a tool for man's purposes. Whether this is for good or evil, time alone will tell.

The pattern of the war's aftermath hardly could have been predicted by any farsighted American.

For while a depression was predicted by economists when the war's demands had been satisfied, it was found that the unfilled civilian demands, in the United States and in war-exhausted nations, lifted the economy to new levels. Unemployment never rose to prewar levels, despite the return of millions of men from the armed forces. The United States found itself helping not only its exhausted friends but its defeated enemies. And the defeated nations, Germany and Japan, recovered faster than any of the victors except the United States.

Unexpected tragedy also followed. For while the war was designed to assure peace, the precarious balance of ideologies and power between Communism and freedom gave birth to the cold war. Instead of lightening the burden of armament from the shoulders of Americans, our expenditures after a few years increased, and the Korean War has seemed permanently to have decreed that we remain an armed camp.

The loosening of the bonds of colonialism over the world has produced a spawning of new nations which have become an international problem of major proportions.

At home, vast and unprecedented changes have taken place in our industry, in agriculture, in the distribution of the population, in the living standards of our people, and in the role of government in our lives.

Measured in terms of 1954 dollars, our gross national product in 1940 was $205 billion. In 1950 it was $318 billion, and in 1959, $426 billion. Per capita, the GNP has increased 60 per cent.

The national income originating in all manufacturing industry rose 600 per cent in the twenty years after 1940; in constant dollars, about half that.

In the electrical industry, with which so much of this book has been concerned, the production of kilowatt-hours of the electric industry increased fivefold from 1940 to 1960. In the manufacturing of electrical equipment the kinds and varieties of usefulness have marched ahead in like proportions.

While in the United States in the years since World War II so much food and fiber has been grown that vast government outlays have been required to sustain the surplus, the number of farms and the number of people who work on the farms have sharply declined. Because of mechanized farming and larger farms, 10 per cent of the farmers grow 90 per cent of farm production. In 1940, 9,540,000 workers were employed in agriculture. In 1959, there were 6,003,000.

The shift in the general population has been from rural to

urban. And in the urban areas the shift has been from the cities to the suburbs and beyond the suburbs. This has greatly changed all political, educational, and other calculations.

The predictions were made and widely accepted in the nineteenth century that, while the United States would grow in total wealth, there would at the same time remain a persistent growth in poverty. But that prediction has not materialized. By all the scales of measurement the American people have almost entirely emerged from the shadow of poverty, and the number in actual need has declined to an almost negligible and irreducible minimum. Hourly and weekly wages have risen to heights undreamed of, and, despite the inflation created in the war and since the war, they buy a remarkably high standard of living. The increase in savings has been spectacular. Individual home ownership has increased, and, despite the immense indebtedness in such ownership, individual investment in homes and furnishings is vastly greater than it was even in the prosperous 1920s.

But it is a remarkable reflection on the American people, and not one which is pleasant to contemplate, that they have shown a progressive affinity for the beguilements of politicians who tell them that their security and prosperity are dependent upon paternalistic government. And this weakness, which was understandable in the depression years before the war, has persisted in the face of the demonstrated fact that the government was so dependent upon private enterprise in the war years. Thus, despite the lift in living standards rooted in the productivity and opportunities in the private sector of the economy, government outlays for relief in many forms have grown to unprecedented heights. In 1940, when there still remained a large number of unemployed and when general prosperity still lingered near depression levels, welfare outlays by all governments, Federal, state and local, amounted to about $9 billion. In 1950 they had grown to $24 billion, and in 1960 to nearly $50 billion. Even deducting from this figure various kinds of social security, which has some of the attributes of insurance, the growth has been enormous.

Inexorably, therefore, the welfare state has replaced the welfare community.

Federal participation in this field has grown faster than state and local participation. It has increased sixfold since 1940.

Along with this assumption by the Federal establishment of responsibilities hitherto resting upon the states and local communities, a vast bureaucracy has appeared. In 1940 there were 996,000 employees in the civilian departments of the Federal government. In 1959 there were 2,185,000. Despite many laudable statements and some real efforts by President Eisenhower to cut down the Federal bureaucracy, it remained about the same until the end of his two terms. And now it is certain to rise to new heights because of the programs sponsored by the present Administration.

What with this burden of government and the erosion of private philanthropic funds by high taxation, more and more are being sustained by fewer and fewer.

Thus, despite the immense growth of wealth and the multiplication of job opportunities, and despite the immense sums spent by public and private agencies in education, the virtues of self-reliance and self-help have notably lost their appeal to Americans. It may well be that we are seeing the fulfillment of the melancholy prediction of Tocqueville, stated in his

Democracy in America one hundred and twenty-five years ago, that the real threat to a free people is the rise of a tutelary state. All this has marked the century in which John C. Lincoln lived. It may well provoke the question whether the principles of self-reliance and individual enterprise, which Lincoln represented so well, will gain or lose in the century which lies ahead.

Chapter XV

AGE DID NOT WITHER

WHEN the second half of the twentieth century opened in 1951, John C. Lincoln was in his eighty-fifth year. There was no curtailment of his many interests and responsibilities. His mind, enriched by so many years of experience in the world of action and of thought, manifested no loss in vigor or acuteness. He was still seeking new outlets for creative enterprise.

In Cleveland the Lincoln Electric Company, which Lincoln had founded fifty-six years before, had reached a major position in electrical manufacturing. Lincoln attended directors' meetings when he was in Cleveland. He and his family were large shareholders. He still visited the Lincoln Electric plant and watched with interest the new mechanical and scientific devices in operation there. The Universal Wire Spring Company was prospering after its years of growing pains, and Lincoln's contributions to its mechanical operations continued. The development of the Bagdad mine was of absorbing interest to him during the months he spent in Arizona. There were also several real estate corporations, in which he had major interests, in Ohio and Arizona.

The eldest of his children by his first marriage, Louise Lincoln Kerr, was living in Phoenix. John Gladden, also by the first marriage, lived in Wadsworth, Ohio.

Lillian was married in 1952 to Carl Howell. They lived for some years in Pasadena. Joseph was married and lived in Scottsdale, where he was proprietor of a shop manufacturing fine stained glass. David was married and lived on Long Island, where he was employed as an engineer in the Sperry Corporation plant.

In the years after 1951 Lincoln acquired various farm and ranch properties in Arizona, the final one in 1954. For these he employed competent managers, and he visited them during the winter months.

In this period Lincoln came to be interested in producing rain over the desert by sprinkling clouds with silver iodide from an aircraft. Charles Barnes was associated with him in this venture. Lincoln secured a patent for the process, and some experimentation followed. The results were disappointing, and the company which had been formed for this purpose was liquidated in 1954. However, the concept lived and as late as 1960 scientists at the University of Arizona were still working at the idea with Lincoln's precise methods.

The pattern of the Lincolns' life continued as it had been since 1931. Their home was in Paradise Valley, not far from the Camelback Inn. Lincoln dictated his considerable correspondence at the Inn. With Mrs. Lincoln at the wheel of the car, they spent many days visiting the various ranches and at Bagdad. They had a house at Bagdad to accommodate them on their regular visits.

They spent their summer months in Cleveland, living at the Wade Park Manor, a hotel which Lincoln had acquired. There was also the regular three-weeks' stay at Chautauqua where they stayed at the Cary Hotel. While there, Lincoln continued to spend the days and evenings attending the lectures and concerts.

In Ohio, as in Arizona, Lincoln was faithful in attending the directors' meetings of the many business and philanthropic corporations in which he had major interests. He was chairman of most of these, and while he was attentive to the discussions of other members, he was expeditious in the disposition of the business at hand.

His attorney in Cleveland was William H. Bemis, of the firm of Baker, Hostetler and Patterson. Lincoln's association with Bemis began in 1944. Together with Frank Snell in Phoenix, Bemis served on several of the boards, representing the Lincoln interests, and as an officer in some.

In the earlier years in Phoenix, the Lincolns were regular in attending productions of the little theater and the symphony orchestra. Later these diversions were less frequent. When in New York, they attended the theater every evening.

Lincoln's spare hours were given to reading. Here his interests were mainly historical, scientific, and religious. He greatly admired Abraham Lincoln, and Mrs. Lincoln recalls that he read with care the ten volumes of Lincoln's life by Nicolay and Hay more than once. On the long train trips to and from Cleveland his reading was lighter fiction and mystery stories. The Lincolns' last major vacation trip was to Hawaii. Earlier they had visited Bermuda and Alaska.

One of Mrs. Lincoln's interests was a small herd of pedigreed goats. Goat's milk became a major item in their diet, and Mrs. Lincoln attributes Lincoln's amazing vigor to the end of his life to this item of nutrition.

Nature's bounteous gift of twenty-eight years after the traditional age of retirement of sixty-five was not entirely due to an inherited constitutional fiber. Lincoln had contributed his share by constant activity, his avoidance of excesses of all forms, and outdoor living in a bracing climate.

Despite the rugged constitution which supported such an incredibly active life for so many years, Lincoln had not been free from bodily ailments. In 1944 he had suffered an attack of pneumonia from which recovery was complete and speedy.

In 1951 his physician and neighbor in Paradise Valley, Dr. F. T. Fahlen, was disturbed at the signs of a very considerable growth in the vicinity of the stomach. It had appeared suddenly and was growing very fast. Dr. Fahlen decreed an immediate operation by a surgeon in San Francisco. Dr. Fahlen's suspicion of malignancy was confirmed. But the operation was successful, and the recovery was speedy. Lincoln soon renewed his many activities.

There was no recurrence of malignancy, but another abdominal growth necessitated four successive operations in Cleveland in 1955. Again, Lincoln returned to his active life.

In May 1959 the Lincolns visited Bagdad for what was to be the final inspection of the operations there before their trip to Cleveland. They arrived on Wednesday. That evening there were commencement exercises at the high school. Senator Barry Goldwater was the speaker. Mrs. Lincoln assisted in preparing the senator's dinner.

The next day Lincoln was busy all morning inspecting the mine operations and the accounts at the office. But he tired in the afternoon and rested at home until 4:00 in the afternoon, when he went back to the laboratory. His illness increased in intensity, and on the following day he was carried back to Phoenix in an ambulance. After a very serious time on Saturday, he seemed to rally on Sunday. By afternoon he was able to occupy himself with the laboratory reports of the Bagdad operation. But his strength ebbed. Six hours later, his long life ended. Mrs. Lincoln, who was at the bedside, recalled that in ten days they would have been married forty-one years.

Lincoln conceived of life as an endless quest for answers. Answers to the mysteries of science and technology, and the search for a richer material life for all. Answers, too, to his wish that there could be a better and more just distribution of the bounties of nature. A realization, perhaps, of the ideals of Christ as recounted in the testaments he studied so long and so well. Perhaps as he contemplated the life to come, in which he ardently believed, it too would be an unending quest and an adventure.

Chapter XVI

THE MEASURE OF THE MAN

THERE are men whose achievements are so conspicuous that by inference alone the genuine personality is forgotten. A mere recital of the engineering, scientific, and business career of John C. Lincoln brings forth the outstanding qualities of untiring drive, insatiable curiosity, the ingenuity of genius and confidence in the validity of his judgments. Such qualities in some successful men carry with them less admirable traits such as impatience with less gifted associates, cold disregard of the feelings of others, and supreme egotism.

The testimony of those who lived and worked closely with Lincoln concedes his possession of the more admirable of the foregoing characteristics but wholly denies the existence of the latter. In the research involved in the preparation of this book John Love and I have been denied the opportunity to talk with most of those who were associated with Lincoln in his early years. For he outlived the great majority of that generation. But those whom we have seen, who were his friends and associates in the last forty years of his life, have been unanimous in testifying to the kindly, tolerant, considerate nature of the man.

The two lawyers who consulted with him and guided him in his legal affairs are William H. Bemis and Frank L. Snell.

Bemis's responsibilities have involved the Lincoln interests and properties in the East. Snell is the senior partner of the Phoenix firm of Snell and Wilmer. He has been concerned with Lincoln's interests in Arizona.

Both were constantly called upon to discuss and advise with Lincoln and his family on many subjects beyond formal legal problems. Both were warm and devoted friends.

In his contacts with these men I noted over and over the significant fact that Lincoln seldom summoned them to him in the fashion of so many important clients. He almost always unpretentiously called at their offices. If they happened to be busy at the moment, Lincoln chatted with secretaries and sub-ordinates, who loved to see him come. And they grew to know and treasure the genuine interest he always displayed in their lives and concerns.

A man of genuine stature is never conscious of superficial measures of relative personal importance. He is assured whether he serves or is served, whether he defers or is deferred to, whether he follows or leads. Lincoln was that sort of man.

Had he enjoyed success as such or the gains therefrom, he could have abundantly indulged in the perquisites of wealth and power. But what has been called "conspicuous consumption" meant nothing to him. Certainly the public note and recognition which might have come from such display would have repelled him.

In Phoenix in his final years his mode of life was in sharp contrast with the evidences of affluence so widespread there. He lived in a modest, comfortable home such as the ones to which he was accustomed in his earlier years. He owned and used automobiles which were neither large nor costly. His dress was what gave him the most comfort for the workshop, the office, or his home.

There are some people, especially in politics, in whom plain living is in itself an affectation. This is for show, mere theater designed for playing a part. But that was far from Lincoln's mind in his habit of modest living. For all vocations in which Lincoln might have excelled, acting a part could not be included. His forbearance in the face of criticism or differences of opinion was not mere tact. It was a real consideration for the point of view differing from his own and his respect for the personality of others. His tireless energy in serving what was important in his life allowed no margin for mere strategy.

The two lawyers to whom he gave his confidence testify to his unfailing consideration for their opinions. Among the business associates who worked with him was Harold Neely of the Universal Wire Spring Company. Their mutual interest in applying the zigzag spring in the manufacture of automobiles required the knowledge which long experience had given Neely. As was noted in an earlier chapter, the engineering of the machinery for the manufacture of the spring required the special talents of three individuals. First Lincoln would project his plan in drawings and operating models. Then Neely would bring the creations to the blueprint stage. Finally S. G. Blumensaadt would direct the building of the final machine.

During his yearly visits to Cleveland Lincoln spent considerable time at the growing Universal plant. There he would manifest the engineer's intense interest in the mechanics of operation. He would talk with the employees, always seeking to learn from their daily operations, making an occasional suggestion but never issuing orders. He was, as one of his associates said, the best of all team workers.

In creating and developing Camelback Inn, he worked in complete harmony with Jack Stewart. Here Lincoln recognized a man with unusual talent in hotel management. Stewart said this after Lincoln's death:

"A great deal of the success of the Inn has been due to Mr. Lincoln's marvelous cooperation and foresight. He was always willing to contribute to the enlargement and improvement of the property. In twenty-three years we never had an argument. He was always calm and pleasant. Also, he was so keen that he could understand the problems of management. He had an extraordinary capacity to come to the point and to express himself with an efficient economy of words. He was without doubt the most intelligent individual with whom I have ever come in contact."

In the many instances in which Lincoln's financial support was paramount he understood the essential difference between ownership and management. He selected his associates with a fine discrimination and then he gave them his full confidence. If there were differences in detail he almost invariably told them that they were the specialists and that their judgment should prevail. The results usually proved the wisdom of this division of responsibility.

When a project failed he was patient and tolerant. He simply liquidated the failure and went on to new ventures with undiminished confidence. No one ever so demonstrated the wisdom of the old saying that there is no use trying "to find a substitute for success." On balance his successes were overwhelmingly predominant.

In his career there were unpleasant experiences which might have justified the development of a hard surface of reserve and suspicion in dealing with people. He had been hurt on occasion by the unkindness or sharp practice of some in whom he placed his trust. But he never repaid such treatment with retaliation. This he accepted as a part of life's experience.

Lincoln's contributions to technology and engineering, highly significant at the time they were achieved, were no small part of the nation's growth to pre-eminence in the world. These will be surpassed and built upon by successive generations. His religious and social ideals may take a long time in getting recognition by a people who are seeking less exalted goals.

But there is something in the life of this man, reaching as it did through almost a century, which has a deeper value to this and the generations to come. Lincoln proved what has so often been called the American dream. Self-help, hard work, unquenchable curiosity, and faith in the ideals of American civilization—these were of the very essence of Lincoln's character. He proved for all to see what can be done by one man in a climate of liberty.

These virtues, like the man who possessed them in such abundance, were not born in the twentieth century. Nor was the conviction that they could bear rich fruit. They are, according to a philosophy which calls itself "modern," old-fashioned, not to say outmoded, virtues. This position is taken by many who are in places of influence, even by many in high, policy-determining, official authority. Once more in a highly sophisticated form a very ancient belief finds root among us, a belief that the individual is helpless unless he becomes the dependent of a higher earthly patron—the state.

But the tree is justified by its fruit, public policy by its results. Sturdy individualism antedates the twentieth century, even the era in which Lincoln was born. And so, it is called "old" by those who count only in decades rather than centuries. But if it be old, even by that short standard of time, it has produced something very, very new. And good beyond all the dreams of the centuries. A better and richer life for all. Higher standards of enlightenment. Here in America a light shines through the world. A miracle of change for the better. And so the "old" has brought forth new fruit.

What sort of fruit can be produced by the "new" subordination of the individual to the ministrations of an allegedly benign public authority we do not know. We are asked, however, to give in exchange for a mere hypothesis something which had proved itself. But if we can count in centuries, we must know that the "new" concept of dependence is not new at all. We are asked to exchange independence for dependence. For we know that far back, even before the gospels were written which Lincoln interpreted with such powerful insight, dependence upon a sovereign authority for individual growth has always ended in frustration and failure. The "new" is not new at all.

But since dependence has become so attractive, it appears as a sort of public philosophy beguiling young and old alike. We may wonder sometimes if there will be another career like that of John C. Lincoln. There are other concepts, which have gained great acceptance, that there are newly invented and easier ways to succeed.

The basic purpose of this account of a man's life may serve, however, as a reminder of what freedom in enterprise, freedom to experiment, room to fail and to rise again, can offer to an individual with the character to grasp his opportunities to serve. Here is a luminous and durable reminder that these freedoms will be neglected by this and succeeding generations at mortal peril to the nation and the world.

Appendix

LIST OF PATENTS GRANTED TO JOHN C. LINCOLN

Item No.	Year	Title of Patent	Patent No.
1	1891	Electric brake	458,587
2	1895	Electric motor	539,277
3	1900	Electric controller	646,526
4	1900	Electric brake controller	661,880
5	1901	Electric drill	676,043
6	1902	Apparatus for curing meat	705,367
7	1906	Operating mine door activating mechanism	829,974
8	1906	Variable speed electric motor	829,975
9	1907	Variable speed electric motor	847,088
10	1909	Apparatus for curing meat	930,772
11	1910	Electric arc lamp	949,151
12	1911	Electric arc lamp	949,081
13	1912	Convertible motor	1,018,833
14	1912	Electric arc lamp	1,031,352
15	1912	Apparatus for curing meat	1,037,941
16	1912	Variable speed electric motor	1,043,325
17	1912	Apparatus for curing meat	1,044,201
18	1913	Electrical reciprocating mechanism	1,050,960
19	1913	Electromagnetic apparatus	1,063,170
20	1914	Brush holder	1,090,159
21	1914	Apparatus for preserving meat	1,102,769
22	1914	Welding metals	1,108,592
23	1914	Dynamo electric machine structure	1,115,947
24	1915	Alternating current motor starter	1,163,424
25	1916	Casting welding electric bonds	1,183,992
26	1916	Bonding railway rails	1,183,993
27	1916	Variable speed electric motor	1,194,645

APPENDIX

Item No.	Year	Title of Patent	Patent No.
28	1916	Portable means for securing the reverse flow of electric currents	1,201,837
29	1917	Electrode holder	1,217,468
30	1917	Method and means for transforming direct current	1,227,809
31	1917	Method of and apparatus for producing sparkless commutation	1,244,518
32	1918	Electrical bond for railway rails	1,261,140
33	1918	Uniting railway rails	1,281,402
34	1922	Means for starting and operating motor generators	1,413,747
35	1924	Stabilizer	1,502,789
36	1924	Arc welding	1,506,374
37	1925	Electric arc welding	1,521,894
38	1926	Mold for cast welding rail bonds	1,581,455
39	1926	Method and means for bonding railway rails	1,581,456
40	1926	Electric arc welding	1,589,017
41	1927	Dynamo electric machine	1,618,962
42	1929	Electric arc welding	1,711,151
43	1929	Flux holder	1,722,929
44	1932	Welding apparatus	1,869,013
45	1932	Arc welding electrode control mechanism	1,869,014
46	1932	Arc welding apparatus	1,869,015
47	1932	Method of and apparatus for welding	1,869,350
48	1932	Method of and apparatus for making pipe	1,869,351
49	1935	Making welding rod or flux holder	2,000,182
50	1937	Apparatus for cooling membrane	2,093,458
51	1942	Wire bending, with W. H. Neely of Cleveland and S. G. Blumensaadt of Cleveland Hts.	2,305 266
52	1951	Vaporization apparatus	2,577,023
53	1953	Apparatus for bending sinuous wire strips into springs	2,632,482
54	1956	Apparatus for preparing finely divided material	2,762,574
55	1961	Spring cushion	2,981,318

Index

Index